RE

Art in Southern California

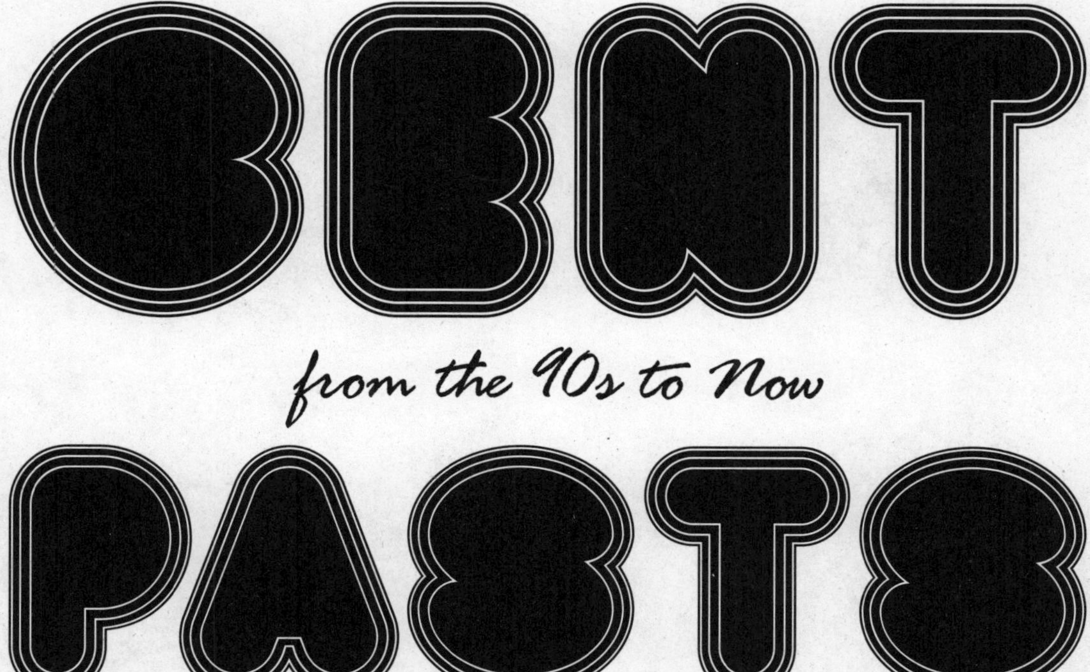

Recent Pasts: Art in Southern California from the 90s to Now

Volume 1 of the SoCCAS
[Southern California Consortium of Art Schools] symposia

Edited by John C. Welchman

jrp|ringier

Table of Contents

Preface

John C. Welchman

On behalf of the Southern California Consortium of Art Schools I would like to thank all those who gave so generously of their time and resources to make this book and our inaugural symposium possible. Our major source of funding came from the art departments and studio programs of the member schools themselves, whose chairs and deans were creatively supportive of our new undertaking: Art Center College of Art and Design, Pasadena (Jeremy Gilbert-Rolfe); California Institute of the Arts, Valencia (Tom Lawson); Claremont Graduate School (Connie Zehr); Otis College of Art and Design (Roy Dowell); University of California, Irvine (Yong Soon Min); UCLA (Barbara Drucker); University of California, San Diego (Steve Fagin); and the University of Southern California (David Bunn).

The Museum of Contemporary Art kindly sponsored our venue at the Silver Screen Theater in the Pacific Design Center in Hollywood, and I'd like to thank MOCA's director Jeremy Strick, Ann Goldstein and Lisa Mark, and the staff in the Education Department, especially Suzanne Isken and Aandrea Stang, for their assistance and hard work leading up to June 2004.

The University of California Institute for Research in the Arts (UCIRA) also assisted us with funding for a grant-writer and logistical support for grant applications.

At the heart of the consortium are two executive committees, one composed of faculty from the member schools, the other of graduate students in the MFA or adjacent MA and PhD programs. Both groups contributed enormously to the programming, implementation, and aftermath of our founding event, so I'd like to thank the faculty representatives: Mike Kelley (Art Center College of Art and Design, Pasadena); Allan Sekula and Sam Durant (California Institute of the Arts, Valencia); David Pagel (Claremont Graduate School); Annetta Kapon (Otis College of Art and Design); Juli Carson (University of California, Irvine); James Welling (UCLA); and David Bunn (University of Southern California).

Special thanks are due to the graduate representatives, many of whom worked tirelessly to help get the consortium up and running by assisting with the speakers, PR, satellite events, and numerous other matters: Michael Holte (Art Center); Fiona Jack (CalArts); Spencer Douglass and May Jong (Claremont); Hunter Woo (Otis); Steven Lam and Amy Robinson (University of California, Irvine); David Hatcher (UCLA); Katie Herzog (University of California, San Diego); and Anna Graham (University of Southern California).

Many others from the schools and wider community contributed to the mission of the consortium, and I'd like to thank in particular: LouAnne Greenwald (USC), Leslie Marcus and David Walker (Art Center); Patti Quill (formerly at UCSD); Diego J. Garza and Enrique Castrejon (CalArts); and Eric Medine.

Lionel Bovier at JRP|Ringier and his colleagues Gilles Gavillet, Clare Manchester, and Lukas Haller have been committed to the SoCCAS series from the beginning and we're very grateful for the vision and professionalism of this innovative young press.

Finally, sincere thanks to the speakers and essayists themselves most of whom did double duty helping to create a memorable day on June 21, 2004, and then went back to their presentations to turn them into the original and wide-ranging essays and position-papers you'll soon be reading. Whatever usefulness or impact this collection has in helping to outline some of the issues and territories of visual art practice in Southern California during the last decade and a half is a testament to the richness of their work, vision, and opinion.

Introduction

John C. Welchman

R*ecent Pasts: Art in California From the 90s to Now* is based on the symposium of the same title held at the Pacific Design Center in June 2004, with the co-sponsorship of the Museum of Contemporary Art, Los Angeles (MOCA). The event represents the first of an annual series of international events organized by the Southern California Consortium of Art Schools [SoCCAS]. SoCCAS is a unique programming body formed in 2003 to promote exchange and engagement between the art schools of Southern California, the wider community and an international audience in the form of outstanding lectures and publications by local, national, and international artists and cultural critics; panels and discussions; and themed mini-symposiums. The consortium also facilitates exchanges between students and sponsors student-run events, including presentations and discussions of current work at various venues. SoCCAS offers an exciting way to headline the extraordinary concentration of art schools in Southern California and cement the identification of this region as a world leader in art practice, criticism and pedagogy.

The founding-member schools of the consortium were Art Center College of Art and Design, Pasadena; California Institute of the Arts, Valencia; Claremont Graduate School; Otis College of Art and Design; University of California, Irvine; UCLA; University of California, San Diego; and the University of Southern California. In Fall 2004 the University of California, Santa Barbara, joined SoCCAS (with Renée Green as its faculty representative).

A faculty committee comprised of representatives from each school developed SoCCAS's inaugural symposium with a view to providing an informal map of key developments in the art scene of Southern California over the last decade and half. We wanted to hear a range of voices from across different artistic communities, including not only practicing artists, but curators, city cultural officials, critics, and a recently graduated young artist from a member school. We also wanted discussion of art contexts outside of metropolitan Los Angeles, where more than half of the consortium schools are located.

Beyond these loose parameters, and a sense of commitment to artists in their early or mid careers, we didn't impose any further conditions on our participants. It soon became apparent, however, that our project had three zones of focus: on new initiatives from within the institutional or commercial sectors of the art world, which we called "Inside"; on developments mostly situated outside of this more sanctioned sphere, whether in alternative spaces or the public domain, which we termed "Outside"; and finally, on innovative art and art-related activities that were taking place in sites, such as the Southern California deserts and San Diego-Tijuana border, that are relatively remote from the culturally dominant LA basin, which we labeled "New Locations." Of course, these sectors were neither discrete nor in any sense definitive. So we decided to program a final panel ("Endpapers") with short presentations by three artists and a critic whose independent thinking and constructively targeted polemic has helped shape art-world discourse in Southern California in recent years. Included here was a recently graduated MFA student, Yanira Cartageña, who chaired the organizing committee for a parallel initiative among the SoCCAS art programs, the group exhibition *Supersonic*, which exhibited work by graduating MFAs from the then eight member schools and opened with great fanfare the night before the symposium.

Cultural historian and regional California aficionado, Norman Klein, plays weatherman for the introduction to the volume. In "The Boost: Cultural Meteorology in Southern California" he meditates on the changing images and self-representations of Los Angeles and vicinity, coupling this with a deeper and more ironic account of how the area's control of many aspects of visual media is interleaved with the enduring cliché's of its own identity: sun and surf, palm trees and freeways.

The essayists addressing developments from "Inside" the institutional and commercial art world of Southern California were chosen because they have both spent significant parts of their careers as writers, curators and artists exploring the hinterland between the official or market-oriented sectors and more alternative forms of art practice and criticism. MOCA curator Cornelia Butler offers a reflection on the changing nature of curatorial practice, mapping the shifts she describes in relation to the ambitious and much-anticipated exhibition of feminist art on which she is currently working, *WACK! Art and the Feminist Revolution* (due at MOCA December 10, 2006, to April 17, 2007). For her contribution, artist and writer Frances Stark offers a personal history of the rapid development of the art scene in Los Angeles' Chinatown, where she has maintained a studio since 1998. Shortly thereafter, Chinatown emerged on the art-world radar with the opening of China Art Objects, and in the past seven years as many as 40 galleries and alternative spaces have opened along Chung King Road and nearby streets and alleys. Stark addresses the layered issues and nagging questions that have informed her Chinatown years: the role of artists in an ethnic neighborhood; the grails of success and legitimization; gentrification; crossovers between art and music; criticism and reportage; and the speculator mindset of many collectors. Stark suggests that the popularity of Chinatown is founded less in a declarative shift in artistic style or exhibition practice, and more in its image potential—whether played out in terms of real estate, utopia, bohemia, art history ... or all of the above.

The second section of the book, "Outside," addressed to art practices located beyond the confines of the gallery, museum, or art institution, is modified slightly from the symposium. For the live event, Julie Silliman, Cultural Arts Planner at the Community Redevelopment Agency of the City of Los Angeles, who is responsible for guiding art projects in public and private developments within 34 redevelopment neighborhoods including Downtown, Hollywood, Crenshaw, San Pedro, Watts, and North Hollywood, described a wide range of public art projects commissioned by her agency (and others) over the last decade. While artists have created public art in Los Angeles for more than a century, it is only in the last 25 years or so that such work has evolved in coordinated relation to government mandate. As more and more branches of government and individual municipalities embrace public art, and it can now be found with increasing frequency throughout the public domain—the art programs—which fueled this explosion, she argued, are largely reactive entities, following changes in theory and practice developed within the disciplines that shape the built environment. Silliman used these determining considerations as the bases on which she grouped and filtered the development of the public art projects she presented—whether temporary installations (such as that by Cindy Bernard and Joseph Hammer inside MTA Metro Blue Line trains; and the humorous fake signs at a park in Santa Monica by the Happy Puddle Collective), or a major, permanent work, such as the interactive electronic project for a new housing complex across from the Staples Center by Cameron McNall.

Paradoxically, the availability of public art to a diverse audience, outside of the institutional context of art viewing, often renders the work invisible to the so-called art world. Silliman examined a range of related issues including how changes in art practice impact what artists create for the public; the relation of sculpture to architectural structure (as in Liz Larner's *Bridge at Walt Disney Studio*, a 321-foot long undulating blue pedestrian bridge in Burbank, or Richard Turner's design of the MTA's Metro Green Line Aviation Station which mimics the neighborhood's aerospace buildings from the 1950s); or how artists are introducing alternative narratives into spaces typically dominated by commercial messages (Erika Rothenberg's *The Road to Hollywood—How some of us got there* infuses quirky tales of personal successes by film industry insiders into the infrastructure of the mega Hollywood & Highland shopping center; while Beep, Inc's [Pae White and Tom Marble] Rapid Bus bus card decals, bus seat fabric designs, bus stop seating and symbols tell multiple stories of romance set among the Boulevards and destinations along the bus route); and, finally, how artists including Robert Irwin, Barbara McCarren, Jacci Den Hartog, and Elizabeth Bryant have used their interest in plants to influence landscape and garden designs.

Unfortunately, Silliman was unable to convert her talk on new practices of public art into written form (she was, understandably, busy becoming the mother of twins!). We therefore invited curator and art and media historian Rita Gonzalez to contribute an essay on recent developments in the Southland's Latino/a and Chicano/a art worlds, one of several key topics that we had originally intended to program but were unable to because of time limitations in the auditorium. Gonzalez's text, "Strangeways Here We Come," thinks through the shape of new work in her community in relation to a series of encounters and discussions between different protagonists and generations, emphasizing that the emergence of new forms and ideas has been a function of intense self-reflection and animated exchange in which many of the stereotypes of Latino/a practice have been simultaneously rejuvenated, recast, and rejected.

For the symposium, artist and DJ Dave Muller gave a spirited illustrated introduction to his work concentrating on the development after 1994 of his signature Three Day Weekends, a series of evolving, nomadic collaborative project spaces conceived and operated by Muller for provisional locations that range from galleries to freight elevators, and generally run for three days on holidays and adjoining weekends. To give a sense of the geographies (London, Tokyo, Athens, San Francisco, New York, among other cites), issues and textures of the TDW phenomenon—which include Muller's notion of "amorphous authorship," and what critic Ralph Rugoff referred to as "territorial trespassing"—we decided to reprint a key interview between Muller and the curator Hans-Ulrich Obrist, conducted in 1998, to which I added a few questions on more recent developments.

In their essay "The Big Squeeze: Micromedia in the Age of Megalomedia," media critic Holly Willis and Anne Bray, the founder and director of the biennial video festival LA Freewaves, trace a history of video art and media production, distribution, and exhibition in Los Angeles within a multi-layered context that includes funding shifts, changes in the city's geography, and the evolution of digital technology. LA Freewaves and other notable projects in media and new media programming in and around Los Angeles in the last 20 years, including c-level (in Chinatown), Art in Motion (AIM) and key new media programs at several schools and campuses, form a cluster of innovations that underline the powerful contribution made by Southern California artists, critics, and curators in these areas of practice. c-level, recently reformulated as Betalevel, is a cooperative public and private lab formed in 2001 to share physical, social, and technological resources with a membership of artists, programmers, writers, designers, agit-propers, filmmakers, and reverse-engineers. Part studio, part club, part stage, and part screen, c-level plays host to media events such as screenings, performances, classes, lectures, debates, dances, readings, and tournaments. AIM was founded in 1999 by Janet Owen and Jim Keller, and originated as a response to globalization of communications protocols, including the Internet, over the last decade or so. Until 2004, it supported digital media artists with an infrastructure—including physical spaces for production and theme-based exhibitions, public education programs, and fora for theoretical discourse within the time-based media community.

Bray and Willis examine these developments in relation to signal changes and realignments over the last two decades: in public and private funding and sponsorship; in technological development; in the art world's shifting relationship to time-based media; and in the second of the "big squeezes" that title their essay, the global compression of time and space.

The third section of the book addresses three "New Locations" for art practice beginning at the southern and eastern edges of California. Curator and critic Osvaldo Sánchez discusses the evolution of inSite over the past dozen years or so and introduces the curatorial concept for inSite_05. Since its inception in 1992, inSite has mapped the intricate networks of permeability and blockage that characterize the border zone of San Diego-Tijuana. Recognized for its importance both as a strategic node of globalization and as a locus for reimagining contemporary identities, the San Diego-Tijuana region has increasingly become a site of extensive critical analysis. Focused on the specificity of the San Diego-Tijuana corridor as a mutant context of unexpected political and cultural rearticulations, inSite's activities revolve around periods of artists' residencies and intricate processes of collaboration and coauthorship. Throughout successive versions of the project, groups of curators and artists have contributed diverse models of practice through which inSite has proposed new readings and added further layers to the region's socio-cultural weave: from IN/SITE92's emphasis on installation art; to an interest in spatial and symbolic context demonstrated by the in situ works of inSITE94; to subtle intrusions in urban space and its public representations in inSITE97; to diverse processes of cultural practice evident in inSITE2000, when works were based as much on events and experiences as on aesthetic products of controlled visibility. Sánchez argues that "Bypass," the theoretical axis of inSite_05, seeks to interlace situations of flux, mobility, and experiences of interconnectedness by bringing together a group of artists and curators interested in "stimulating the gestation of new utopias of belonging and dynamics of association within the public domain." inSite_05 presents a "connective topology that links the mobility of urban networks with the cultural displacements and symbolic transformations of urban identities in flux."

In "A Guided Tour of the Center for Land Use Interpretation [CLUI]," the experienced expeditionaries Matthew Coolidge and Erik Knutson present a history of the CLUI, founded in 1994, by unfolding an annotated map of the complex territories of the Center's activities—public tours, exhibitions, publications, archives, databases, and site-specific extrapolative work in the field. Since its inception, CLUI has set its sights on marginal or overlooked landscapes and outposts, operating at the borders of science and at the edges of the art world. Crossing the liminal and the well-trodden, remote locations and urban centers, working "under the radar" from a nondescript storefront in Culver City, yet operating on multiple fronts or sites, and garnering national attention, CLUI epitomizes the subtle renegotiation that characterizes one strand of recent art in Southern California between new social and geographic terrains.

The contribution of artist Marcos Ramírez (ERRE) and architect and theorist Teddy Cruz, "Zero Art in TJ" contextualizes recent cultural, urbanistic, and social developments at the geographic, political, and artistic boundary between Tijuana and San Diego. As *San Diego Union* critic Robert Pincus notes Ramírez "has been one of the most trenchant observers of border culture for several years." His public art frequently challenges the boundaries assumed by social relations and charges them with historically-conscious irony. ERRE's project for inSITE97–a 30-foot Trojan Horse brought to the San Ysidro border—was the work of what Mike Davis called "a consummate magical realist." For his part, ERRE suggests that geographical and political boundaries are ultimately about the private individual at the border of the public: "Chicano artists often have a problem of feeling they have left their culture behind. They learn a new language but forget the old one—and that's sad. It's good not to forget anything. Instead of feeling half Mexican and half American, I feel double."

Cruz and ERRE also take us on a tour, but this time through the improvisational vitality of Tijuana's hydrid socio-architectural space. They introduce us to a spectrum of householder-designers from the barrios to the new middle-class, who deploy such a bewildering array of found and recombined materials, appropriational tactics, and belligerent ingenuity that the metropolitan art world's more mannered versions of similar gestures begin to look a little staid.

The symposium concluded with short presentations and a panel discussion between three Southern California artists, Meg Cranston, Daniel J. Martinez, and Yanira Cartageña, who were joined by critic and curator Malik Gaines ("End Papers"). We have preserved the spirit of this roundtable by asking the panelists to present a brief position paper based on their remarks in the Silver Screen Theater. Cranston's "Building a Better School: A Corrective Rethinking of the Concepts" is a modestly iconoclastic proposal for rethinking the whole idea and purpose of the art school. Bursting the bubble of the vaunted reputations garnered in the press by various SoCal schools over the last decade or so, her tongue-in-cheek manifesto dismantles the magna dicta of the growth-oriented art academy arguing against fundraising, bigger buildings, ever more equipment, and cornucopic student subsidy.

In "We Are All Conservatives ... or ... We Are Dogs in Love With Our Own Vomit," Daniel J. Martinez raises the stakes of Cranston's irony with a zestful polemic launched against the complacent branding of what he terms "global corporate conceptualism." For Martinez, 21st century artists have an obligation to confront their social confusion and make work in the space between "art, radical politics, and radical theory." Chair of the steering committee of MFA students drawn from the eight member schools, Cartageña's "One wind tunnel, Eight schools, 120 artists" is a candid view of the process and effects of the *Supersonic* exhibition hosted by Art Center, Pasadena, in the giant Wind Tunnel space at their new south campus. Organized and installed by the MFAs themselves, this initiative resulted in what is probably the largest and most ambitious group exhibition of graduating art school artists ever attempted, and drew commentary from the regional and national press. Offering a participant point of view, Cartageña examines the process, successes, and limitations of the show, noting that it did much to promote exchange between the schools, managed to avoid stamping students with campus-specific

IDs, and, most importantly perhaps, that by virtue of both its democratic lay-out and design and the critical orientation of particular contributions, *Supersonic* was more of a showcase for the creative diversity of genres, styles, and approaches to art-making in the eight schools than a kind of "emerging art fair"—as predicated by some observers.

Gaines' "Theater of the Repressed ... or ... All I Got Was This Lousy MFA" discusses a number of Southern Californian art practices, including *Beat of the Traps* (1992), a collaboration between Mike Kelley, Anita Pace, and Stephen Prina, and work by Catherine Sullivan that ranges across the intersection between performance, theater, dance, and music—"working in the inderdiscipline," as he puts it. Gaines (who participates in the collaborative band/performance group, My Barbarian, as well as writing criticism, performance scripts, and other textual forms), argues that an "expanded pedagogy" is needed on the part of the art schools to keep in check the centrifugal pressures of calibrating success according to market validation or generic delimitation.

Allan Sekula was unable to participate in the symposium, so we have added to "End Papers" a brief essay by him, "Facing the Music." It was published on the occasion of an exhibition of the same title, curated by Sekula for Gallery at REDCAT, Los Angeles, April 14–May 29, 2005. The exhibition included photographs by Anthony Hernandez and Karin Apollonia Müller; a digital installation by James Baker; and Billy Woodberry's DVD, *The architect, the ants and the bees* (2005); as well as Sekula's 18-minute DVD *Gala* (2005), and slide projection piece, *Prayer for the Americans 3 (Disney Stockholders)* (1997/2005). Using Frank Gehry's new Disney Concert Hall on Bunker Hill in downtown Los Angeles as a focus, Sekula returns to the issue of civic boosterism discussed by Klein, reminding us of all that is marginalized or occluded by the master-narratives of high-brow cultural achievement—whether measured in human, infrastructural, or environmental terms.

The Boost: Cultural Meteorology in Southern California

Norman M. Klein

I have been inhabiting the Southern California "art school world" for 30 years now—through seemingly endless variations of post, neo, and retro. When I first arrived, the ghost of the Pasadena Museum of Art (1954–1974) was still being mourned, along with the loss of downtown art schools like Chouinard (founded in 1921). There were still hippie remnants filtering through the California Institute of the Arts, Valencia, just north of LA, where I teach. One of my first students claimed that he was channeling aliens, who told him that they had trouble understanding my lectures.

Then came the art cycles, from Pop and Minimalism to Conceptual and Installation and on to Video and New Media. The 1970s boom in alternative spaces paralleled the growth of west side art galleries. After 1980, many new museums were added in Southern California. And with each of these moments, like the recent flourish over Frank Gehry's Disney Concert Hall, came fierce hyperbole, in the press, in conferences, in catalogs—saying that this time, LA had definitely taken off: It had finally become "world class." I learned at the same time that only two cities in the world always presume that Southern California never has enough "class:" New York ... and Los Angeles itself.

I had always presumed just the reverse, that LA was a tortured "world class" mess, a fascinating case of nervous distemper. I am obsessed by its microclimates, its self-denial, and its powerful cultural calamity. As an historian, I see no problem comparing it to Paris of the Second Empire, or London, or Vienna in the 1890s, because I know what massive foolishness gave those cities their cultural energy. It is inspiring to watch the world about to explode, just out your window, and to be absorbed by the epic problems of the local.

In Southern California the local has often been treated as an embarrassment. Presumably we need boosterism and flashy glamour to cover up how essentially empty we are. This is not necessarily true at all, another myth. However, the struggle to wallpaper over "our emptiness" is the very energy that drives culture here. Too often Southern California treats itself as a chain of prairie towns pretending to be garden cities—something like Kansas with attitude. Meanwhile, to the world at large, this is a dynamic laboratory for the next century, not because it runs so well, but because it runs in all directions at once.

What is more, almost everyone I meet feels marginalized here. We all become that clerk at the dry goods store watching the big gunfight a mile away: witnesses off-screen. That makes for a yawning disconnection between the arts and media/booster marketing—all that incessant hype, intemperate glamour, and their empowerments. We in the arts each get a dainty taste, but no one feels invited. The anxiety is fascinating. Equally fascinating, and more important, the overlapping of ethnic cultures here is as epic as in New York a century ago. We are indeed the new Byzantium; and over the next thirty years, when the population of the LA basin will probably double, the region will undergo a profound political transformation, be caught up in vast water wars, and witness a fetishistic new constitution of its inner cities. In the end, it will probably feel, once again, as if we are were watching the world about to explode; and generate more of that tentative, peevish, disengaged version of urbanism that makes the arts here unceasingly ironic, and continually uneasy.

So I vote for the so-called mess that is already here and growing: the odd neighborhoods, the layers of ethnic difference. I am convinced that Southern California can generate new forms for the emerging catastrophes that face our nation. And, very likely, once these forms actually emerge (probably "below the radar"), the leadership in Southern

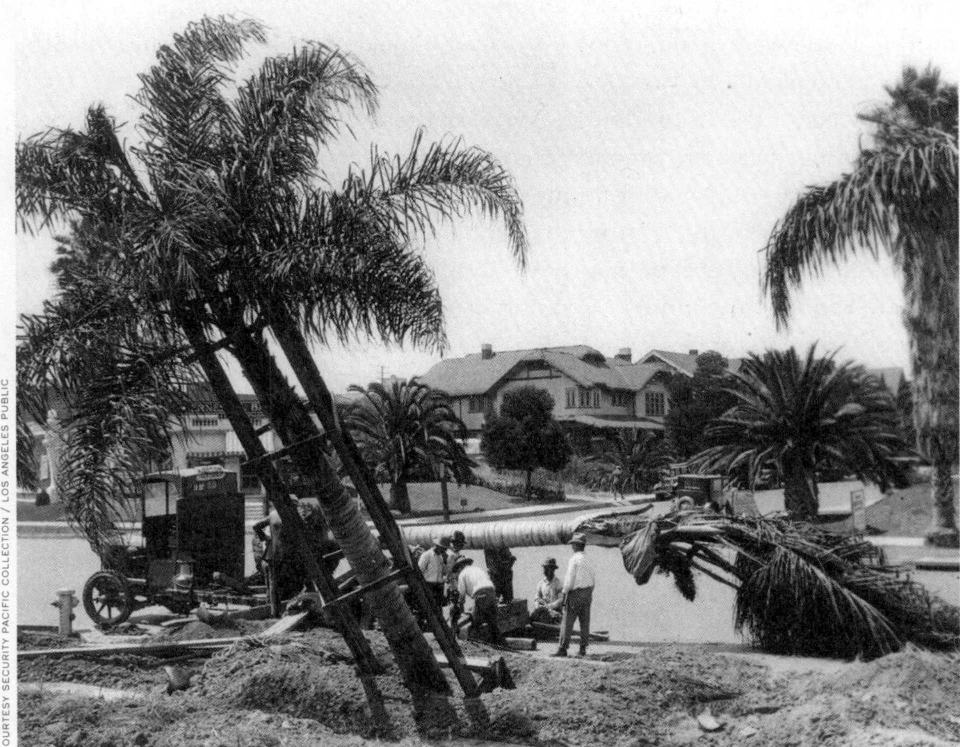

COURTESY SECURITY PACIFIC COLLECTION / LOS ANGELES PUBLIC

Tree Planting on Wilshire Boulevard, 1926
Two full-grown palm trees are being planted along Wilshire Blvd. between Western and Wilton.

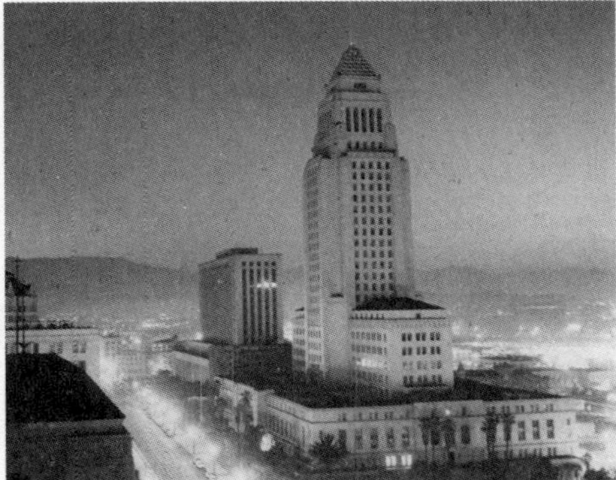

COURTESY SECURITY PACIFIC COLLECTION / LOS ANGELES PUBLIC LIBRARY

Los Angeles City Hall, 1955
View of Los Angeles City Hall the evening of February 22, 1955. The clock in the *Los Angeles Times* newspaper building in the lower left forground reads 5:45 p.m. and the sky to the right of the City Hall tower is lighted as the result of a nuclear blast test in Nevada.

California may still fear that we are not "world class" enough, and that all this localism is a sign that we are still hicks putting up a cheap motor hotel in the middle of the 1920s.

My role here is to identify some of these "climate shifts." Or should I say, the climatology, that exhaustive term invented by Carey McWilliams back in the 1940s, when it suggested a broad connection between boosterism—the marketing of the city—and the mild weather itself. As early as 1890, the culture of Southern California specialized in merchandising its topography and unusual microclimates (the Mediterranean and Switzerland only acres apart). For the arts, the story often begins with the Arroyo School between 1890 and 1920, which was a partner (along with the *Los Angeles Times*) in boosting (even huckstering) the "all-year-round" weather. Art promised, then revealed, a utopia, from the canyons to the beachfront. Much art criticism back then mystified the climate as well as the real estate. It promised a non-hierarchical "arts" alternative to the East Coast. Here the rustic and the modern somehow coexisted. It was a farm town with modern roads, Kansas City with attitude; literally, because the Santa Fe railroad plied directly west from Kansas City. In Southern California you could pretend that none of the gruesome inner city calamities were anywhere in sight.

It was a glorious nonsense that generated many illusionistic, scripted spaces—set up in a world that never had much of a public sector, and certainly nothing like the palaces, museums, and industrial hubs of eastern and European cities. As a result, privacy seemed to repave the city streets themselves—replacing public urban rhythms like nowhere else in the developed world. Southern California also had seemingly unfettered wealth, and was, at the same time, a workingman's paradise. Presumably there was room for all classes to exaggerate their need for glamorous privacy, refreshed by ocean breezes, or cleansed by the dry, health-giving heat. Presumably there were no urban cultural boundaries, just your version of experiencing the climate. Here you were free to invent your own nervous breakdown, which happened time and again in noir literature and film, and from the Beat Generation to the new art scenes of the 1960s and after.

Of course, climatology was mostly an evasion—though I still remember dozens of newcomers over the past 30 years who arrived to avoid a winter, then stayed forever, as if their internal clock was stuck. They kept waiting for something like winter finally to arrive, to tell them that they were actually aging. In the meantime, they started working out with free weights, getting liposuction, building an imaginary youthful body. They started to look as if they slept in an oxygen tent, or spent their days floating in a pool of rare oils. They began to internalize the miraculous disaster of climatology, in a culture designed for hiding out.

These myths about eternal climate as psychic damnation were reified further in cinema, design, architecture, the fine arts, even in graffiti. While much of this myth dissolved in stages after the first Watts Rebellion in 1965, some strains are still with us: a neo-Kantian version of the sunshine as sublime, apparent in the writing of critics such as Dave Hickey, Jeremy Gilbert-Rolfe, and even the *Los Angeles Times* art pundit, Christopher Knight. I remain, however, a committed neo-Marxist skeptic, a happy dinosaur watching us all (myself included) try to hide from the era of Bushismo. Anyway, none of these ideological differences mean that much any longer, as I will suggest in a minute.

As 2004 turns into 2005, the arts in Southern California present a culture dominated more by ethnographic complexity than by climate, by emergent “post-border” theory as the larger collapse begins, and the next blend of Latino and Anglo capitalism gets underway. Key also are new modes of urban alienation—and the shocks of our current political crisis. And at the same time, of course, much that is still climatological lingers on, like a designer spirituality shrouded over the art world. My prejudices are clear; better to be honest than hide them. I am an old-fashioned Baudelairean modernist, obsessed with ironic, surgical engagement; even a structuralist trying to invent new forms of media narrative. So I am generally less interested in the artistic (sublime) version of boosterism that never seems to go away in Southern California. But the reason for its eternal return fascinates me. Through its boosterism, Southern California has pioneered since 1890 what has since become the globalized entertainment economy, from tourism to branding to Hollywood to “lifestyle” marketing. Here, illusion and simulation have been instruments of power for over a hundred years, essential to our cultural history.

So I try not to argue why certain art-specific works are beautiful. Better to summarize the broader facts of the matter, the social history of the arts since 1974. I am a cultural critic. As a cultural critic, I do best when I write about the historical envelope, leaving my eccentric, sometimes perverse, art tastes out of the way. I prefer to elaborate on the myths of climate, essentialism, and boosterism as social history, and leave the reader to decide which artists assimilate, reformulate, or critique them.

What are the new versions of climatology as of 2005? What cultural shocks are transforming how art will be made and received (or deceived)? Southern California is the center of vast trans-national shifts, a kind of "tectonic" ethnography. As a result, while massive shifts overwhelm our fiscal, political, and economic systems, we live "in the stomach of the dragon," culturally speaking. For example, I often say that the one place where movie glamour doesn't work is Southern California. Everyone knows a tortured soul working like a galley slave in "the Industry." Everyone has had their street blocked off by a pack of raving Visigoths calling themselves a movie crew. We keep seeing famous actors without makeup, ravaged by the latest drug rehab; or smiling oddly after the last plastic surgery, as if a rubber band inside their cheek might snap while they crawl through the aisles at a supermarket—the movie star's real face before the next round of skin erosions.

As a result, there is also a glibness to our simulation when we pretend that we are insiders, or if we pretend that we are utterly marginalized. It is part of the group theater of Southern California. We applaud too much, and we worry about looking negative. However, behind all this mental subterfuge, this psychic gymnastics, we Southern Californians know that hoaxes are real, because we watch them literally being made. Speaking for myself at least, underneath the slick attitudes we are still in the grips of art as climatology, perhaps now more than ever. So, as an historian of public confusion and bad memory, I will invent a little drama about this recurrent problem: first act, climatology as it is in 2005. Dénouement: how it will evolve by 2030. Along the way, I leave the reader to fill in the blanks, maybe using the ideas and art practices discussed in this book. You can best decide which art objects are revealing and which seem to hide. I'm talking more about the weather.

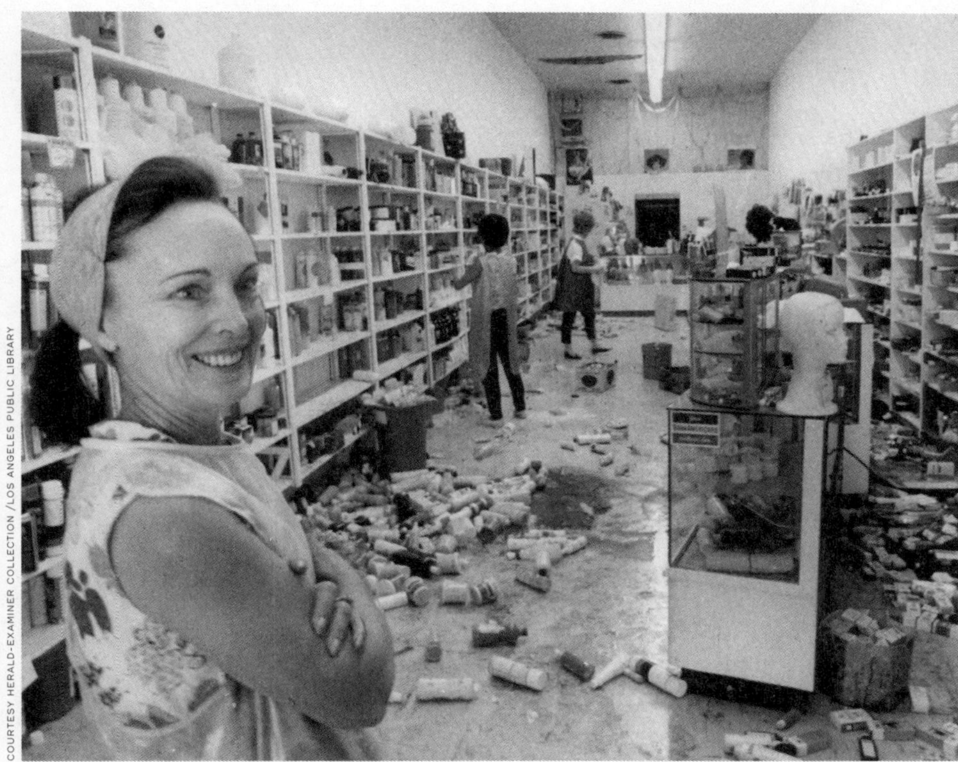

COURTESY HERALD-EXAMINER COLLECTION /LOS ANGELES PUBLIC LIBRARY

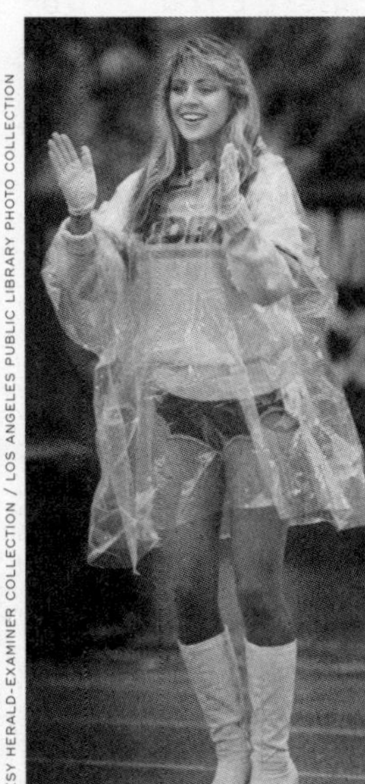

PHOTO: JAMES RUEBSAMEN
COURTESY HERALD-EXAMINER COLLECTION / LOS ANGELES PUBLIC LIBRARY PHOTO COLLECTION

Earthquake Damage to Beauty Shop, 1971
Mrs. Edna Merritt of Pacoima and other employees of the Crown Beauty Shop, 1032 San Fernando Road, San Fernando, grind away at the awesome cleanup task posed by hundreds of broken bottles of perfume and hair dye. The photo was taken when the job was already half-done. Workers noted they had the sweetest and most colorful floors in town.

Cheerleading in the Rain, 1985
At the Raiders vs Broncos game, cheerleaders still remained beautiful in the rain.

1. The Professional Artist During The New Dark Ages

In the 8th century ACE, many scholars and artists hid in monasteries to avoid the collapse of Europe. There they copied Latin manuscripts, in what was later called the Carolingian Renaissance. In the US since the 1960s, artists, poets, critics, and others have increasingly turned to universities and art schools for sanctuary, as the older distribution systems for culture have been dissolving.

The court is still out on whether this professionalization of the experimental in the arts will ossify or nourish our culture. But it is certainly reinforcing a broader trend that cannot be shaken. There is no point in hating—or glorifying—this trend, as its momentum (or entropy) is relatively unstoppable. I call it "the hollowing out of America," or the "horizontalizing" of culture (power pulling horizontally, away from the central government, even away from the continental United States). Almost all vertical systems for art have slipped, and the routes to fame are more obscure than before. The twentieth century ranking of cultural capitals, venues where artists can make an international mark, and the premier journals where scholars and critics make someone famous—including sometimes themselves—are also being short-circuited or reversed.

While the second Bush administration continues its rapturous campaign against blue states like California, other trends will be worsened: funding for the arts, for example, will shrink statewide and citywide. Parallels to the Bushist cultural decline will become evident in other nations as well, particularly in Europe. We will see a fracturing of the old stairway to fame, resulting perhaps in a new Carolingian Renaissance, a revival of the great pressure to hide and copy. This must be resisted.

Nonetheless, resisted or beloved, the role of art schools will increase enormously, as the public sector for the arts suffers. Eventually, an avant-garde might exist inside a five-square-mile radius, flourish, innovate, and remain unknown elsewhere. That may be splendid and healthy. But how will art schools in Southern California nourish what the broader art world may increasingly ignore? Our myths (or at least my myths) about the inevitability of "good" art may be challenged further. And how will the hierarchical, sometimes stodgy, nature of universities and colleges be offset to allow new forms to emerge out of this professional/academic art system. These are some of the challenges that the Southern California Consortium of Art Schools [SoCCAS] and the joint graduating exhibition of June 2004, *Supersonic*, are clearly trying to address. How successfully, time will tell. But the "monastic syndrome" will certainly grow during the coming decade. We must look forward, not nostalgically backward, fashioning the art school into a public realm for new work, with even more determination than we see now. Southern California has clearly been a leader in this professionalization since the early 1970s.

2. The Age of Real Estate Apartheid

At the moment, one of the most popular topics of discussion is this: when does the current real-estate boom finally collapse? It is very likely that within the next few years it will loose its fizz—and probably loose more than fizz. But the social isolation of economic classes, based on real estate and a dozen other factors, will increase. A Manhattanization of the beach towns and west sides of Southern California has already taken place. Arts culture is rapidly shifting further inland, toward areas that are much more ethnically and socially mixed, like Highland Park or East LA. That will continue for the next decade, as dozens of new galleries, music venues, alternative spaces of various kinds appear. Artists are increasingly redefining themselves as independent entrepreneurs, who run small curatorial venues. But again, as I mentioned earlier, this should not be seen as just another symptom of some neo-avant-garde. The dynamics that made avant-gardes so powerful a century ago no longer exist in our cities. The bohemian romance of becoming that was central to modernism is past. Southern California will find a much more horizontal version of cultural experimentation, more about ethnic niches, about internet exchange and "below the radar" forms of culture, from art on post-it scraps to instant video cinema. This new culture on the nickel will be fresh, sometimes very raw, but surely a helpful sign. Look, for example, at *The Rambler*, an innovative little sub-zine published in Chinatown, LA—just one of many new distribution systems for "alternative" or "underground" artwork (if those terms still apply today).

Also, work achieved on and near the border in San Diego/Tijuana remains vital, and important. We should expect to encounter microclimates for cultural experimentation in the Inland Valley, particularly in parts of Orange County, the eastern San Fernando Valley, and across much of the eastern areas of the LA Basin (east of La Brea, but particularly east of Western). I look forward to being surprized by where in Southern California new forms will materialize.

One crucial point: even more than the real estate buzz (another notorious boosterist obsession), there is endless debate about how the Latino plurality/majority will "take over" in Southern California. Indeed, that is inevitable, but not in the apocalyptic way that the media usually portrays. New York did not turn into a Yiddish Poland, or New Sicily, around 1950. Instead, it became a colossally important cultural amalgam. The same will be true of Southern California, which is emerging as something quite unique—not simply Mexican, or Salvadoran, or Chinese (mainland or Taiwanese), or Korean for that matter. Imagine a new species of ethnic culture altogether. So when we discuss new microclimates being formed in the arts, we should see them as a newly innovative form of urban civilization, as well as new approaches to old problems, including the massive poverty that will afflict recent immigrants and older residents alike. We are being forced to invent a new door to a structure that does not exist yet. Our culture lacks the terms even to describe it: can there be a place that is neither private nor public; neither intimate nor exposed; not global or local, a migratory blur that isn't blurry at all; and not simply digital, because now the computer is invading "real" space, literally digitizing in city streets? Young artists are crucial to this bizarre transition, however dangerous the process may become next. With no easy answers offered, they must be taught to see the emerging ethnography as a hopeful and prescient moment—with more than enough material for new forms of engagement in the arts.

3. Entertainment Economy

Southern California helped initiate the consumer-driven art of the 1960s and 1970s, LA Pop, Minimalism-lite, and so on. But much of the Pop heritage, filtered through conceptual art and its aftermath, assumed something that no longer exists. It assumed a barrier between consumerism and high culture. Today, that barrier has dissolved. The entertainment economy has absorbed much of the fine arts. It simply happened; no one is directly responsible, unless you want to blame Rupert Murdoch (I'm always ready to blame Murdoch, and the media distribution stranglehold that his image conjures up). You could blame the rise of digital entertainment. Or you could blame the realignment of cultural and trans-national business since the end of the Cold War. But we must face up to the political and cultural "aftershocks" (to use a local metaphor) of Southern California's confrontation with a civilization where entertainment practically drowns out the other arts; or relies on them as critic and incubator for new forms.

So the next few decades, certainly the next few years, will be a test of nerves. Can the professionalized art-school world adapt to the end of postmodern difference, and locate a powerful new grammar for a globalized culture in a context where entertainment has overwhelmed practically everything else. Even 30 years ago, there were still constant references to literary and historical memory in arts discourse, in classroom discussions, and among those engaged in public culture. Now, to be utterly objective, one finds little or none. Our collective memory has morphed into entertainment and media. This is our Latin, our French, our post-structuralism, our toolbox for looking backward or forward.

Entertainment, of course, tends to be very conservative, despite its hipness and wowness. New forms are only new bottles. The distribution system and the huge corporate investments leave no room to retool—any more than the auto industry is prepared to retool for a new kind of car. So under the radar, and inside our microclimates here in Southern California, the new possibilities will be hatched. I guarantee it. If not here, then where? But will those in charge of art worlds increasingly linked to art schools and universities find a method for reconstituting arts education to meet the challenge? Time will tell. This book must be seen as one attempt to make this restructuring possible. New forms require new systems of production and cultural theory. I leave it to readers to locate their own possibilities in what follows.

It has been raining fiercely this week in Southern California. The great tsunami disaster of December 2004 has just struck South Asia. The weather is undoubtedly different as you read this. But the climate probably has not changed all that much. Please update my suggestions. For the next few decades, every year may feel strangely foreign to the next, as this horizontal dismantling and reinvention moves along.

Inside

LA, Now and Then

Cornelia Butler

I was born and grew up in Los Angeles, left and swore I would never go back, knew that I would, finally did, and am only now beginning to understand the vast gift of being a cultural worker in a city that is always about change and inhabits its clichés with a comfortable bravado that challenges even the most cynical visitor not to love it. In some ways my curatorial destiny brought me full circle to the city around which my undergraduate thesis revolved: *A History of Artist Museum Relations in America*, I grandly wrote in 1984. Beginning with the foundation of the Museum of Modern Art in 1929 and culminating with the exemplary Museum of Contemporary Art, Los Angeles, exactly half a century later, in 1979, I traced the unique relationship between artists (not works of art) and the institution. Giddy with the simultaneous experience of being the first curatorial intern at the fledgling MOCA, intoxicated from painting the floor of what was then the Temporary Contemporary for Michael Heizer's installation (as trustees, it seemed, waited outside the door), or happily trapped inside Maria Nordman's airless Santa Monica apartment for weeks sorting negatives for a book that was never to be published—these were my formative curatorial moments, and working with living artists was what I wanted to do.

Returning to MOCA years later with a better understanding of the history of Los Angeles and its cultural institutions, it seems to me now that a history of curatorial work on the West Coast reads much differently than might a similar effort in New York. The reasons for this have as much to do with geography as anything else, especially the spatio-temporal reality of the city itself. The perception and the reality here is that one is, in some way, liberated from history or at least the Euro-American version that dominates the way the past is understood and produced on the East Coast and in Europe. There is the issue of space. Studio space and artistic practice evolve differently in a place where artists and real estate aren't as symbiotically entwined. In a review of Paul Schimmel's *Out of Actions* exhibition, *New York Times* critic Roberta Smith said that such an exhibition could not take place in New York because of an institutional lack of will rooted in the different relationship to space—ambition and curatorial convention tied to real estate and its lack. I'm certain that the exhibition I am now planning, *WACK! Art and the Feminist Revolution*, which opens at MOCA in 2006, would never originate in New York. A spatial reading of the origins of the feminist art movement on the East and West coasts yields profound differences in the way the movement evolved and how artists participated in it. But there is also something to the challenge of available curatorial real estate that makes one think grandly about exploring wildly fraught historical territory and reclaiming it for the West Coast.[1]

Opening to the public in 1984, Frank Gehry's Temporary Contemporary initiated a new kind of museum architecture. The real estate deal which enabled the police car garage to be transformed into a generative example of adaptive reuse for museums—MASS MoCA, Tate Modern, and DIA Beacon are much later examples of the same idea—could never happen in a city such as New York and certainly the origin of such a rethinking of museum space in Los Angeles is significant. And the space itself has influenced a generation of important historical exhibitions in which MOCA curators have ambitiously wrangled with large chunks of post-war art history. The museum has built an international reputation on these large survey exhibitions, the scale and scope of which elude the institutional ethos of its East Coast counterparts. Basically, exhibitions such as *A Forest of Signs: Art in the Crisis of Representation* (1989), *1965–1975: Reconsidering the Object of Art* (1995), and *Out of Actions: Between Performance and the Object, 1949–1979* (1998) could only happen in Los Angeles. This is true, in part, because these

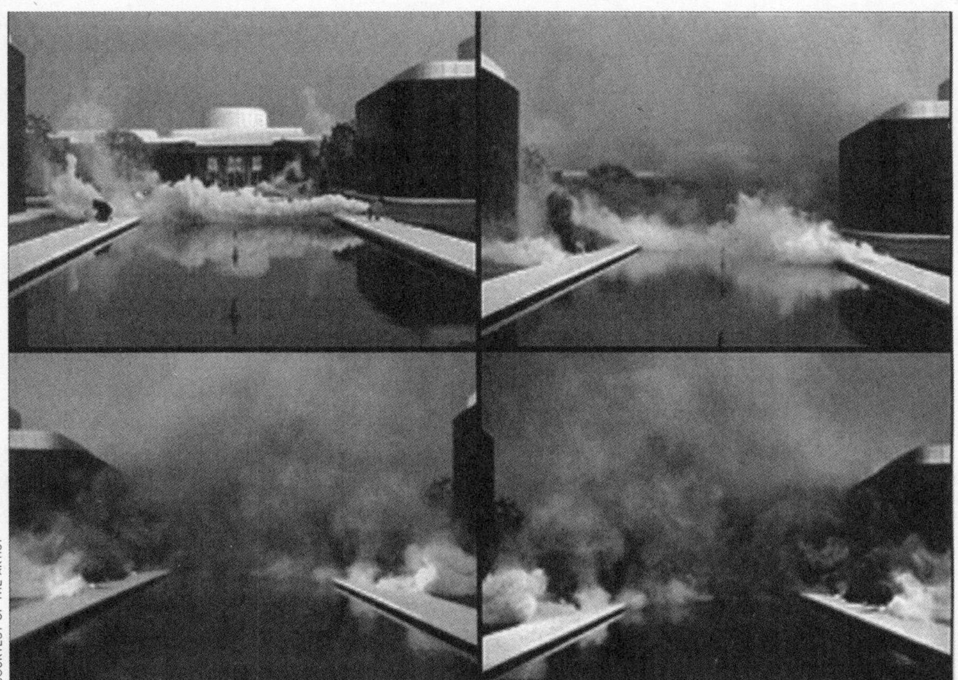

COURTESY OF THE ARTIST

Judy Chicago
Multi-colored Atmosphere, 1970
Video documentation of performance
at Norton Simon Museum, Pasadena, CA

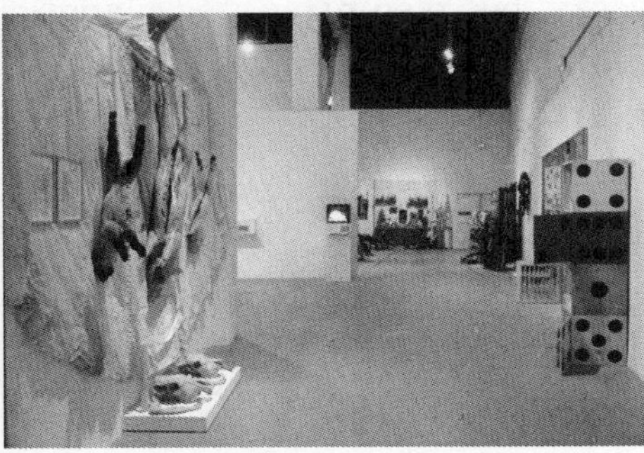

PHOTO: BRIAN FORREST
COURTESY THE MUSEUM OF CONTEMPORARY ART, LOS ANGELES

Out of Actions: Between Performance and the Object, 1949–1979
Installation View
The Museum of Contemporary Art,
Los Angeles, 1998

exhibitions were conceived to redress the lopsided accounting of art on this coast. *Reconsidering the Object of Art*, for example, a survey of Western conceptual art from 1965–1975, reinserted the crucial role of California conceptualism into the cannon of East Coast conceptualism, this underlining the importance of artists such as John Baldessari, Allen Ruppersberg, Bas Jan Ader, Bill Leavitt, and others. What remains to be done is a closer study of West Coast conceptualism, which engages such tropes as humor and language in ways that might be understood as uniquely regional.

What I'm interested in is if and how the place and space of Los Angeles and its premier contemporary art space impact the curatorial process. Certainly the disjunctive and nomadic practices of curators such as Hans-Ulrich Obrist, Okwui Enwezor, or the team at inSite in San Diego/Tijuana are informed by the institutions and cities from which they operate. How does being more institutionally bound both to a museum and city that has the odd distinction of being simultaneously provincial and intensely international affect the exhibitions that are made here? What kind of exhibition-making does the almost utopic open plan of the Gehry building encourage? Given new museum architecture such as the Kanazawa 21st Century Museum of Modern Art—a collection of individually articulated gallery spaces within a large open space—how can the open plan be used to reconstruct new models for the international exhibition?

This last question is on my mind as I begin to consider how my upcoming feminist project will occupy that beloved space that is now the Geffen Contemporary. When MOCA mounts historical exhibitions, part of its self-proclaimed mandate has been to ask the question about how and if California or Los Angeles figures into a given history. For example, the recent Robert Smithson exhibition not only de-emphasized the artist's contribution as an inventor of Earthworks, but also attempted a spatial understanding of the landscape of the west and how it impacted his overall practice and his evolution from New York Minimalist, to the invention of the non-sites and the process-based pours and flows which dominated the later part of his career. The fact that this exhibition originated in Los Angeles is also worth mentioning. If no New York institution was willing to organize this exhibition of perhaps its most influential and radical artist of the post-war period, does this betoken a kind of resistance to claim him?[2] But I digress ...

Feminist art as we know it in North America originated in Los Angeles not far from MOCA's Geffen Contemporary in Little Tokyo and very near Chinatown, where, in recent years, one of the most interesting and fresh gallery enclaves in the city has sprung up. "Chinatown," as it is known, is an amalgam of artist-run, commercial exhibition spaces, a kind of 1970s construction resurrected in the current Los Angeles scene. One of feminism's inventors, the artist Judy Chicago, claims that part of the institutional resistance to feminist art is fundamentally connected to its origin on the West Coast.[3] I'm certain this is true and I get a chuckle thinking about how the East Coast academy will eventually deal with the *Dinner Party*'s arrival at its unlikely roost, the Brooklyn Museum, where it will be on permanent, unavoidable view in its backyard. In broad strokes, what distinguishes West Coast feminists from their East Coast counterparts is that even as their sisters in New York formed cooperative galleries and agitated for parity in an art world dominated by men, the ladies in Los Angeles, unmoored from a commercial art world that simply didn't exist on the West Coast, were busy re-envisioning nothing less than complete social change from the ground up. In the spaces of the CalArts Feminist Art Program (truly a suburban hinterland in the years around 1972), the Women's Building near the geographic center of Los Angeles, just east of the Geffen Contemporary, and *Womanhouse*, not to mention on the campuses of Irvine, San Diego, and Fresno, women came together to make art and reinvent their lives. Part of the project of *WACK!*, as I see it, is to integrate these histories with an internationalist reading of parallel feminist practices and simultaneous feminisms.

As is often the case with Los Angeles, the task is to reread the history and dislodge the monocular vision of its claim of authorship, i.e. LA didn't really invent feminism but rather functioned as a kind of greenhouse for ideas that were percolating throughout western and central Europe, Latin America, Canada, and the post-colonial outposts of Australia and New Zealand. Whether expressed as collective activity or, as was more often the case, individuals finding their way to liberation in isolation, women were interrogating identity, introducing subjectivity and generally intervening in cultural hierarchies of all kinds in ways that fundamentally changed the way we see and profoundly altered the way art is made.

I am, for instance, interested in how Los Angeles artists Suzanne Lacy and Leslie Labowitz's collaborative, public performances evolved as much out of the CalArts Feminist Art Program as they did from a long history of activist performance going back to the social sculpture of Joseph Beuys. Lacy has often spoken about how her formative work of the early 1970s was informed by Allan Kaprow and the legacy of the Viennese Actionists who were present in California at the time. The very ambitious, international programs of spaces like the now defunct Los Angeles Institute for Contemporary Art [LAICA] not only supported the performance work of emerging artists like Chris Burden and Paul McCarthy, but also imported artists such as Ulrike Rosenbach from Germany and the Italian artist Gina Pane, then living in France. Rosenbach also taught briefly at CalArts and remembers the hostility she felt from the Feminist Art Program's pedagogical style and what many people saw as a limited range of subject matter and formal possibility. Many LA artists who were defining their practices even as feminism was transforming their lives, found support through venues such as LAICA and the gallery space at Irvine. Barbara T. Smith, among others, remembers feeling validated as an artist by the 1973 conference at CalArts at which hundreds of women came together to share images and life experiences. It is these kinds of histories that complicate and reframe the narrative of feminist art's roots in Southern California. While many of these artists have been recuperated by revisionist histories of conceptual and performance art, the thread of feminist art practice has yet to be articulated and fully integrated into the narrative of post-war art on either coast.[4]

The question of recent curatorial practice as it relates to the subject of feminist art is one that is not as clearly bifurcated East and West. If one considers the project of *Womanhouse* (1972) and the collective activities of the Women's Building which continued until the late 1980s, as early exercises in something like collective curatorial practice, it is clear that the collective activities of *Utopia Station*—the ongoing, multi-sited, nomadic project spearheaded by Hans-Ulrich Obrist, Molly Nesbit, and Rirkrit Tiravanija—is one of several legatees of feminist art's dismantling of the institution. These early efforts, which were free to grow in the liberating territory of California, have their legacy much farther afield. Always alert to "the movement at the edge of the frame,"[5] the women artists practicing in Los Angeles in the 1970s redefined the frame itself.

Notes

1
Roberta Smith, "When Art Became a Stage and Artists Actors," *New York Times*, April 5, 1998, Section 2, Column 1, p. 40. MOCA's recent Robert Smithson exhibition (2004) was important, in part, for similar reasons. The exhibition specifically sought to reposition Smithson in relation to the West Coast, and to reconsider the importance of his experience of space in the West and how it influenced his later career.

2
That the Smithson exhibition was extremely difficult to place in a New York venue has, I believe, everything to do with the peculiar hybridity of his work. Certainly his relationship to the recent past, and particularly a New York-centered version of art and institutional history is evidenced in his writings from early on.

3
Chicago claims there are three reasons for the persistent resistance to feminist art: its West Coast origins; the fact that women make it; and its subject matter, which she sees as always content-based and explicitly centered on the nature of women's lives. I agree with her first two claims, but hope that my exhibition will take issue with the third.

4
While I am focusing here on Los Angeles, this kind of omission is certainly true of other centers of activity such as London. While the recuperation of feminist artists—as opposed to art—has happened in the United States through the 1990s generation of artists such as Janine Antoni, Robert Gober, and others—this kind of acknowledgement has not happened for the British. While there is a strong lineage of feminist practice leading up to the so-called Young British Artists generation, most of these artists seem completely to have repressed it. The work of many of the English feminists has been reclaimed by several recent exhibitions on conceptual art, film etc., such as *Live in Your Head: Concept and Experiment in Britain 1965–1975* organized by the Whitechapel Art Gallery, London, in 2000.

5
This is Peggy Phelan's term; see her introduction to *Art and Feminism* (London and New York: Phaidon, 2001), p. 17.

A Little Untoward History: On Chinatown's Recent Influx of Art and its Potential

Frances Stark

This essay was originally billed as "First Draft: Toward a History of the Chinatown Art Scene." I have to thank John Welchman for inviting me to attempt it, and for titling it, when I failed, in time, to achieve the lucidity necessary for a title. "First Draft" is a great disclaimer, if indeed either a need or expectation exists for a complete chronology of what has been happening, art-wise, in LA's Chinatown since the late 1990s. With some trepidation, I begin by saying mine is not a paper that pushes steadily "toward a history," but instead, a personal account that may stutter in the "toward," if not becoming altogether untoward. I should remind you that I am not an historian, but a glass-is-half-empty artist. What makes matters worse is that I have been utterly dogged by the feeling that whatever I write is sure to leave any number of Chinatown insiders disappointed or annoyed. So, first, my apologies to all the galleries who have been seriously and consistently mounting exhibitions: Acuna Hanson, Black Dragon Society, Mary Goldman Gallery, Happy Lion, Daniel Hug, David Kordansky Gallery, Sister, Peres Projects, 4F, and sorry to all of the alternative venues like 100 Times Better, Electronic Orphanage, PruessPress, The Barber Shop, c-level, and Mandarin, whose combined energy and enthusiasm have produced more than I could ever begin to assess in these few pages; and then of course sorry to all the many artists, architects, and entrepreneurs I don't mention, who are just as embedded in Chinatown as I am.

I couldn't play the role of a spokesperson if I tried, and I don't intend to assume the role of a narrator either. My discussion evolves primarily out of my relationship to China Art Objects Galleries, as their project has engendered questions and problems that have both inspired and plagued me over the past half decade. In the interest of full disclosure I should say I married into China Art Objects, in fact I was literally married in that gallery to Steve Hanson, one of its founders.

Beginning in 1999, newspapers and magazines repeatedly spotlighted Chinatown's gallery phenomenon, and the *LA Weekly* has taken the pulse of the Chinatown gallery scene a few times over the spread of about three years, but all that reporting does not exactly send the message that a movement is afoot, or a profound change is happening in art that shouldn't be missed. Rather, it seemed to boil down to pointing out a hotspot, a neighborhood on the verge of gentrification, dispatching the tip, don't-miss-it-while-it's-still-charming-and-cheap. This goes for the artworks as well as the property values. Everyone knows artists "fertilize" real estate, even *The Wall Street Journal* pointed out Chinatown on the gentrification radar in September 1999; and they struck a tone that seemed to mock the artists, making them appear paradoxically childish and elitist, punctuating their article with the quote, "I would be very bummed if a Starbucks moved in." It's as if they were saying get ready to be bummed, irrelevant losers. There's still no Starbucks, and as much as people like to point the finger at tousle-haired, stuck up, whitey and charge "gentrification," it is pretty clear that any increase in Chinatown property value is a drop in the bucket compared to many other of Los Angeles' east side neighborhoods where prices have escalated tremendously.

Gallery Row

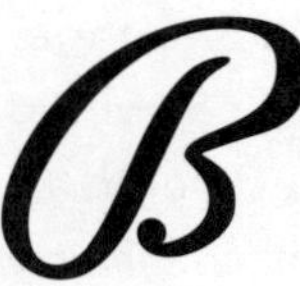

ecause of all this "potential," Chinatown breeds busybodies who want to know who is doing what and with whom and why; they want to know how they are being perceived, and how much this building costs, and what that landlord did.

They want to know if things are going to change and if that change is going to affect them. Will my rent go up? Will I be kicked out? Is there another building I should buy? Was I misrepresented in that article? Is that newcomer going to ruin my vibe with their disagreeable taste? Six years of this type of chatter and anxiety has muddied my perspective. Surely this is not unique to Chinatown; I guess it's the downside of being on the inside. I've let my bad attitude off the leash a bit, because I was hoping some of these issues, petty as they sound, could broaden my own understanding of what it means to be an artist in LA today, which is actually really rewarding, and maybe even made sweeter on account of LA, the actual city, being so hostile toward contemporary art. Let me give you an example. You know those blue and white signs around LA with the city seal, the ones that say Silver Lake, Atwater Village, Miracle Mile etc.? A new one was recently unveiled—"Gallery Row"—only a stone's throw from The Artists' District and Skid Row, though I'm not sure if Skid Row has a sign or not. If you want to know the exact point at which the history of Gallery Row begins, that's easy, because on the Gallery Row web site it states very clearly that on June whatever, I forget the date, of last year, so and so and so and so, I forget their names, submitted their proposal; the point being that the history was precisely located at the exact moment these three people submitted their idea as a proposal. Gallery Row, they say, seeks to "encourage the growth of creative businesses, create a year-round art market, and give creative people another reason to relocate to Downtown Los Angeles."

A sense of dutiful open-mindedness and curiosity drove me to the opening-day festivals, but I had to stifle my cries of disbelief when I actually saw the sign there in a rather desolate stretch of Spring Street. I guess I've gotten used to thinking of the layout of LA in terms of these signs, call it naiveté, city pride, what have you. LA has been a city of boosterism for so long, so it should have come as no surprise that Los Angeles would officially pretend to care about art in the service of real estate. Bureaucracy and its bogus, bullet-point-able goals in the name of progress could never make sense of the thriving galleries of Chinatown; the fact is you can't understand that market and its value system in civic terms. This clash of understandings—whether it be through daily interactions with shop keepers about their utter consternation with regard to our curious work habits, or through the Business Improvement District's attempt to piggy back on the "cultural" events of the galleries—has persistently played into my reading of Chinatown, posing more social or class questions, more questions about the role and status of artists than the actual work they do.

Two vaguely acquainted employees of Pasadena's Art Center College of Design library, both artists—on what seemed like a permanent hiatus from art making—ran into each other at a moon tribe desert rave and bonded. Together they traveled to more desert raves and there, in the sage brush, at dawn under a full moon they eventually hatched the ecstasy-fueled idea to open a gallery called Expressions. Was that name supposed to be silly and ironic or were they flirting with an attempt to harness an overflowing utopian audacity? In late 1997, when Steve Hanson and the late Giovanni Intra told me they wanted to open a gallery, they didn't even mention the potentially embarrassing "Expressions" and still I expressed doubt as to whether or not they were really up for the practical duties required to do such a thing. I questioned whether they wanted to spend their days sorting through unsolicited slides or making uncomfortable phone calls, but they weren't thinking about running a business, and my practicality-obsessed nay-saying fueled them. In the spring of 1998 they took me to 933 Chung King Road and showed me the space they were signing a lease for. Then and there I changed my tune and instantly set about finding a studio to rent in the neighborhood.

Expressions, it seems, was too idealistic to become a reality. Steve and Giovanni eventually had to bring three other people on board in order to finance their project: Amy Yao, a walking alternative-music encyclopedia and Art Center undergraduate student; Peter Kim, another Art Center undergraduate who was frenetically utopian but also served as the link to the oh-so-necessary money man, his landlord at the time, an accountant in the entertainment industry, the affable non-art-world-based Mark Heffernan. This was an instant community by necessity that would begin fracturing within a year. Being an artist, I was sort of a community of one; I rented my little storefront, cleaned it up, and began my work, alone. And here I want to try to tease out the meaning behind making the distinction between my solitary practice and their decidedly socially inclusive efforts. What I think put China Art Objects on the map, which in turn put Chinatown on the map, was their uncanny ability to couple artistic personae together in a way that produced inadvertent

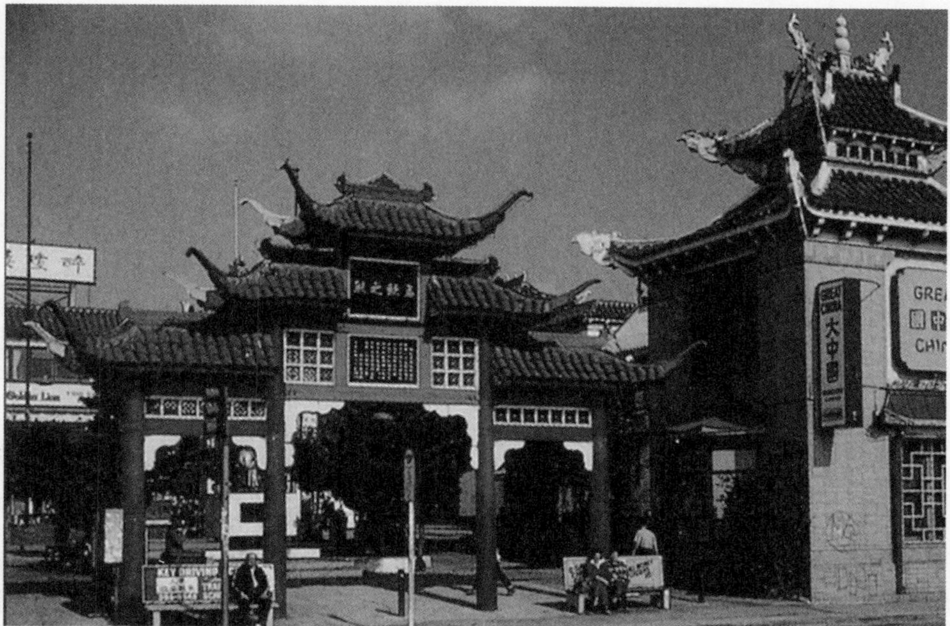

IMAGE COURTESY OF FRANCES STARK

Chinatown postcard with Black Flag Graffiti

collaborations that cut a path into the past as well as the future. I believe this was possible by way of an almost unlikely collaboration between Giovanni Intra and Steve Hanson.

In 1991, at opposite sides of the Art Center library circulation desk, Steve Hanson, an Art Center drop out, and I, an MFA student, had one of our first bonding moments over a mutual respect for the punk band Black Flag. It was Steve's involvement with the punk scene between 1979 and 1981 that acquainted him with LA's Chinatown. Being only 12 years old at the time, I missed out on it, but I wish I could have been there. This kind of wishing implies the scene harbored a movement worth belonging to. I didn't get into punk until 1981, in San Francisco, which means I missed the Chinatown boat. Nevertheless, the punk movement totally affected my life, it gave me an education, a vocabulary of criticality, introduced me to art; it inspired me and gave me something to believe in; so I've given a lot of credence to the punk rock roots of Steve's efforts in Chinatown. Misplaced or not, it makes me wonder why the differences between 1979 and 1981, punk-wise, are tremendous shifts in styles, while the differences between 1999 and 2001 art-wise, are simply tremendous shifts in prices. Forgive my nostalgia and cynicism, but I have had to unearth the punk connection, as it seems to be a paradigm I'm still operating under. I have a picture, obviously printed in a high-school photo class, of Steve and his sister running down Chung King Road, circa 1979, presumably on their way to see Black Flag, X, or The Urinals. The Chinatown shopkeepers have occasionally mentioned the time of the "punky rockers," the punk rock invasion that had as its epicenter The Hong Kong Cafe on Gin Ling Street. It sprouted just as the 1940s Chinatown began to decline, as a substantial wave of Chinese immigration in the 1970s accompanied a subsequent population shift to cities like Monterey Park and Alhambra. In a certain mood, I might even say that Black Flag's performance on the *Decline of Western Civilization* (1981) soundtrack, some of which was recorded at the Hong Kong Cafe, is much more intense, urgent, and paradigm shifting (if you will), than anything you can find in a gallery on Chung King Road today.

This is a song Steve and I have listened to many times lately, a song I listened to a lot when I was a sophomore in high school. I really wanted it to serve as the opening quote to this text, but I thought that was a bit premature.

Reject yourself, reject yourself
and your family of ideals
—the muddle in your head—
You're playing with the reality of the dead
Reject yourself, reject yourself
Built up from scratch
ideas jerry-rigged skeletal tear them down
throw them on the pyre
light it, burn it
rip out your heart, place it on the top
rip out your heart, place it on the top
and
move
to
Antarctica
—100 Flowers (formerly The Urinals, circa 1981)

Back then I didn't know that 100 Flowers used to be The Urinals and that they were coming out of the dorms at UCLA, even though I was corresponding with a friend, Kevin Sullivan, in the art department at UCLA at the time, whose frequent letter writing was busily catching me up on other things like Duchamp, Marxism, how the band The Gang of Four got their name, and stuff about the band Savage Republic. The distance between the style of The Urinals, "arty" but still fast punk, and Savage Republic, "arty" but rhythmic and industrial, is a distance one fluent in the music of the time would gauge as chronological: after punk one would then proceed to a more sophisticated experimentation, along the lines of Johnny Rotten's switch from Sex Pistol's lead vocalist to Public Image Ltd. lead vocalist/idea ranter John Lydon. And this was all done in the space of one or two years. By the way, I should point out that the name 100 Flowers is taken from a saying from the Maoist Cultural Revolution, "Let 100 flowers bloom and 100 schools of thought contend." (Given China's current world-shifting spasm of capitalism I'd say it's okay to indulge yourself; go ahead and wax nostalgic about communism.)

Another lingering notion from the punk era is the term "poseur." As a punk rocker one was automatically posing, stylistically declaring certain allegiances. Think of Poly Styrene's line "I am a poseur and I don't care I like to make people stare." At the same time "poseur" was also a word used to gauge authenticity. There was a critical eye involved, assessing the cumulative stylistic decisions of a person and determining if that person is authentic. Are there significant consequences for lacking authenticity? Now either I have a lot of nerve going here in an academic symposium, or I forgot everything I learned in art school or both, but this internalized judging mechanism warrants attention. What are the standards by which we can gauge authenticity? The vocabulary of artistic style, of aesthetics, seems to have dwindled; if we all share one we don't put it to use much. Is that because it isn't useful? Sometimes I am full of shame for not practicing rigorous verbal specificity. I remember once at a panel discussion that had to do with the crisis of theory in LA's MFA programs, a lengthy round of pontificating on the meta-theory-deprived-situation from the panelists prompted Jeremy Gilbert-Rolfe to brilliantly and sadly burst the bubble by saying, in effect, that nobody had actually referred to a single "art theory" all evening. Was that comic, or tragic? There certainly aren't any publications or critics that have rallied behind even one single gallery in Chinatown. Aside from being disappointing this can also be liberating, perhaps a little too liberating, in that it generates a sense of great responsibility to declare the reasons for taking oneself and one's work and the work of one's peers so seriously. This is a responsibility easily shirked, though, and there's always the market to gauge whether or not what you're doing matters to people.

I met Giovanni in 1997 when he was writing a review for *Flash Art* about an exhibition I was in with two young and prominent artists at the time, Laura Owens and Sharon Lockhart. I mention this because the premise of the show was somehow driven by a desire to see if our interconnectedness as peers and close friends could become perceivable, readable, and relevant; like, could we be linked together under one term, say, the fill-in-the-blank-ists? We collaborated and struggled, trying to get closer to that. The project that resulted interested Giovanni greatly as a critic, and through our discussion of it we became friends. He wrote that our "cryptic show" did not seek a miraculous cohesion, and that our experiment "was an investigation of friendship and location in Los Angeles, thereby turning the celebrity model of collaboration on its head." I had almost forgotten he wrote that until I pinpointed when we met, but it's a nice coincidence because I wanted to mention a few of the early China Art Objects Galleries' somewhat upside down celebrity collaborations. About a year or so into the opening of China Arts, Paul Schimmel's exhibition, *Public Offerings* at MOCA, defined an era of art in terms of career trajectories. The exhibition title says it all, of course, with the stock market buzzword (IPO), and "going public," and its inherent reference to an artist's monetary value, or investment potential.

Around half of the LA artists represented in MOCA's *Public Offerings* exhibit did collaborative shows at China Art Objects in the gallery's first year. The commercial galleries that represented these big ticket artists were happy to oblige, and didn't necessarily see China Art as their competition—and it wasn't a problem, because they didn't manage to sell much of that work anyway. In fact they only become marginally solvent once they began selling things at very low prices by extremely prolific younger artists like Jon Pylypchuk and David Korty. China Arts hosted the first party in their space, timed to coincide with a Christopher Wool opening at MOCA, and Motionsick, a club organized by the artist Kevin Hanley at Chinatown's Grand Star. It was a showcase of sorts, held amidst a freshly shed ten-foot pile of rubble. It would take about five more months before they would open the gallery with their first "real" exhibition.

This inaugural show consisted of a single collaborative work by Pae White and Steve Hanson who had been friends from the aforementioned punk rock period. Pae designed the space, and the gallery realized her design, and then exhibited a fish tank Steve and Pae made that was the gallery in miniature, showing its three levels and its distinctive colors and lighting features, complete with underwater inhabitants that turned out to be mortal enemies. The aquarium showcased their space and underscored their decisiveness about making the gallery look a certain way. I think you can even read it in terms of gentrification. For six months the space was slowly polished until it was no longer rough. The rental property was rehabilitated at no cost to the owner with labor performed and paid for out of a sheer desire to see something look exactly right. A following show paired the well-established Sharon Lockhart with the much lesser known photographs of George Porcari, another Art Center librarian, who was one of Sharon's teachers, and who was very influential in terms of his interests in cinema.

There was also a posthumous collaboration between Bob Weber and Jorge Pardo. This exhibition had Pardo literally highlighting a major unknown influence. Bob Weber, who died of AIDS in 1994, was a close friend of Pardo's. They lived in a loft downtown in the late 1980s and Bob shared his wood shop with Jorge and introduced him to furniture making. In conjunction with the event the gallery also put on a "celebrity" roast, with Pardo in the hot seat, and Steve Hanson as a very Johnny Carson-like MC. The spirit of comedy and entertainment from an era when it was cool to be an old person—a bit seasoned and bawdy—poked fun at Jorge's art world celebrity (he had just finished building a house as part of a MOCA exhibition) with twists on old standards like "when Jorge sits around his house/sculpture he really sits around his house/sculpture." I even had the opportunity to deliver a few tasteless jokes needling Jorge about his recent break-up with the artist Laura Owens, another *Public Offerings* star who mounted a collaborative exhibition at China Art. In this exhibition, the by now well-established young painter, Owens, collaborated with her studio assistant and good friend Scott Reeder, one of the many transplants from Chicago that Laura helped to establish in Los Angeles. Here they divided the gallery into heaven and hell. Their two major paintings were built to just fit into the spaces and one depicted an Edenic bird-inhabited tree; and in the dark basement a subterranean scene, showing moles and other burrowing animals and insects in a maze of dirt, illuminated by candle light. In "hell" they set up a poker table they had constructed to accommodate at least one full night of heavy drinking and gambling. The collaboration amplified the awkward humor that was already at work, but perhaps purposefully ignored, in Laura's already incredibly popular oeuvre. By allowing for the more boyish and directly comedic and cartoonish strategies of Reeder to seep into the market-induced sanctity of her picture plane, Laura had managed to foreground an economy of influence. And by bringing her assistant's signature to a hand that was already at work in the first place, collectors who had been fighting over access to a Laura Owens, a lot of which contained paint applied by Scott Reeder, no doubt now found themselves backing away nervously from something that bore his signature. The invitation to gamble speaks for itself.

Another posthumous collaboration of sorts was between father and son, the late sculptor David Von Schlegell and his son Mark Von Schlegell.

This is a show I wish Giovanni had written about. He has written about several contemporary sculptors, like Liz Larner, John McCracken, Evan Holloway, Isa Genzken, and Andy Alexander, and this particular show was contemporaneous with the somewhat scene-defining sculpture show at the Santa Monica Museum curated by Bruce Hainley. David Von Schlegell was an incredibly prolific sculptor from the late 1950s until his death in the early 1990s. He also headed the Sculpture department at Yale. The exhibition was organized and mounted by his son, Mark, who had recently relocated from New York to Los Angeles, with his then-wife, fellow writer Veronica Gonzalez, now married to Jorge Pardo, and former girlfriend of Steve Hanson. In the main gallery were small wall works in wood and metal that were of significantly smaller scale than everything from David Von Schlegell's entire career, made after he had become sick with cancer, thus cushioning the enormity of what one was about to encounter by way of a group of elegantly ambiguous pieces. In the kitchen of the gallery hung a poster for the artist from Pace gallery, a bizarre anachronism that forced one to reconsider a different era of heavy metal. Pardon the corniness there, but Steve has often joked that the upsurge of ambition among students pouring out of the thriving grad programs the late 1990s were in some ways like the 1980s flood of hair bands on sunset strip, with so many people feeling the climate was ripe for success, creating a huge influx of hopefuls. Downstairs, mounds of career ephemera were carefully but casually displayed, mostly black and white photographs showing massive urban projects like giant plaza installations in collaboration with I.M. Pei. One couldn't help but wonder what the hell happened to all that steel? And how does it, exactly, bow out of fashion?

And so that is just the tip of the iceberg as far as China Art Objects is concerned. The phrase "Chinatown art scene"—this essay's impetus, no less—has consistently diverted me from dutifully adopting comprehensive objectivity. I have, perhaps unconsciously, confused the word scene with the word movement. If there is a movement, it certainly isn't clear to me what the movement is other than the culmination of movements of a growing population of people trying to eke out an existence in any number of vaguely defined layers of a so-called art world. It was unlikely I could pull all of Chinatown's different art spaces under one historical umbrella, let alone even deal with one single gallery's full output, unless I were to construct a one-to-one scale history.

Supposedly, a detailed history of Chinatown's art scene has already been compiled by Joel Mesler. Here's what I wrote about Joel in an article on Chinatown I was invited to contribute to *Index* magazine, in 2002:

> Today there are at least seven galleries and two clothing boutiques on Chung King Road. The quick development has made different people uneasy at different stages. I personally got anxious early on, when rumors circulated that a very young artist was poised to purchase the building that housed the Chinese shop "As You Wish." Ironically Steve and I now rent an apartment above the former store, which has become the Diane Pruess gallery. Its young proprietor, Joel Mesler, whom I avoided meeting for over a year, is now my friend and "landlord." (He hates it when I call him that.) He's also turned out to be the reigning Chinatown diplomat. He seems to know and care about almost everyone in Chinatown, and has managed to bring together a lot of disparate personalities via his irresistible enthusiasm, which he emits with an intoxicating (and/or intoxicated) giggle, excited hand gestures, and mad scientist finger wiggling.

Joel Mesler is no longer my landlord, because he sold the building. I guess that's the sort of thing I was anxious about before ever meeting him. One night Joel was tending bar at Hop Louie's and Steve was listening to some guy going on about the rising property values of Chinatown and the guy wanted in and asked Steve if he knew where he could get a hold of a building, he was willing to pay around 500,000, and Steve sent the guy to Joel, as a joke, since Joel is always complaining about Chinatown wannabes. Before long, Joel was offering the guy his building (which housed our apartment), which he had purchased for somewhere around 250,000 only two years prior. The eager buyer wanted to turn our apartment into an art loft, so as part of the purchasing contract Joel had to ensure we would vacate the property immediately. We thought it was a bit ironic that the person buying the building wanted to live the Chinatown fantasy of being an artist but was so adamant about dislocating us without haste. Now originally I shied away from mentioning this because I didn't want to drown you in a sea of anecdotes, and of course I'm leaving a lot out, but there's something about this particular set of circumstances that warrants a bit of uncomfortable directness on my part. As tenants in the Diane Pruess gallery building, the amount of money Steve and I paid for our rent pretty much covered Mesler's mortgage, making him able to live in and run the gallery space below us with no overhead, no pun intended. This meant that I was acutely aware of my contribution to the scene—which in order to keep the money flowing, meant I had to be a party pooper when it came to the Chinatown pipe dreaming about schools and general stores and soup and sandwich speakeasies. I often felt that the kind of quotidian pressures of my art career were somehow in direct conflict with this art party happening at my front door. So we assumed the expense of a hasty relocation with infant in tow, and he pretty much doubled his money on Chinatown real estate. I think the real issue here, for me, has to do with the crisis of legitimacy and that is too long and hard a discussion to undergo, but should, perhaps, be re-considered in terms of Giovanni's assessment of my exhibition with Laura and Sharon, and Lane Relyea's assessment of that assessment in the *Public Offerings* catalogue: either the trivial glue that holds people together isn't necessarily worthy of critical judgment, or it is precisely the political in the personal and cannot be avoided. The nostalgia for a time when criticism reigned and had a decisive authoritative role that laces that essay is a bit contagious, and not unlike my nostalgia for The Urinals, Black Flag, or Gang of Four which seems to be at odds with the historical self-consciousness that hungers for a certain resolution in the moment. Relyea's text showed a certain contempt for the exhibition that it sought to discuss, and said, in a way, "I'm out of place" or even, as I felt out of place in an academic symposium delivering this text, not because I lack any academic training, though it may appear that way. I feel out of place because I basically decided to talk about what it feels like to be "fertilizer" for real estate, which not surprisingly, is shitty.

Postscript

Giovanni Intra died on December 17, 2002, one day before I was due to give birth to my son Arlo at our home on Chung King Road. This was an accidental death and came as a tremendous shock to everyone involved. Giovanni's last piece of writing was memorialized by the artist Isa Genzken in a recent exhibition of hers at China Art Objects Galleries. The text was about Isa, and because she loved it and appreciated it, she reclaimed it as her own, in a sense, and turned it into a piece that was made in an edition for a Kunsthalle in Germany, the kind of thing those institutions ask artists to produce at the end of the year as fund raising devices. It was pretty remarkable to see the text Giovanni slaved and struggled over simply reprinted and ascribed a monetary potential it never had when he was alive. Giovanni worked insanely hard as a writer and as a gallerist and lived like a pauper.

Outside

This interview between critic and curator Hans-Ulrich Obrist and Dave Muller (b. 1964) was conducted in 1998 and published in the catalogue for the exhibition Wahlverwandtschaften, *Appenzel, Switzerland (curated by Obrist), the same year. I added a few questions to bring the conversation up to date.* JCW

Three Day to Today

Dave Muller in Conversation
with Hans-Ulrich Obrist (1998)
and John C. Welchman (2005)

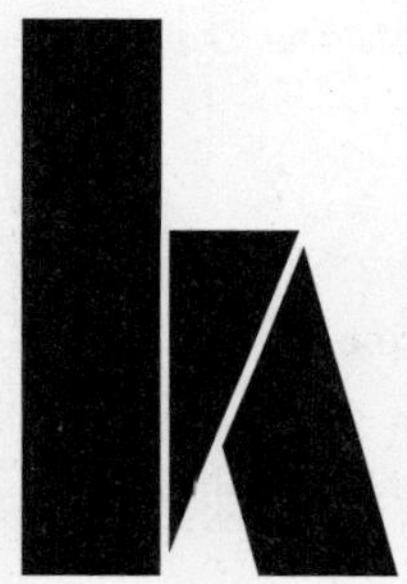ANS-ULRICH OBRIST *How did Three Day Weekend get started?*

DAVE MULLER When I was in graduate school at CalArts, I met with a visiting artist, who ended our discussion with, "Oh, I've got to go, I have nine more meetings." I realized she would see more work from my fellow students in one day than I had in the past two months. The next day I posted a sign-up sheet that read, "On November 14, Dave Muller will be conducting studio visits ... "

During the summer of that year, the school had built a new suite of art studios. As a second year grad student, I won first choice of these in the studio lottery. When I looked at this immaculate new space, it occurred to me that I could transfer all the things that I had in my old studio to this new one, or I could move all my stuff home and use this space for something else. I opted for the latter, and made my studio available to my peers as an exhibition/project space. The most successful experiment was a series of one-day shows. Anyone could sign up for a twenty-four hour slot, and every day was different for four weeks.

After I graduated from school I moved into a loft in downtown Los Angeles. I wanted to continue in the spirit of these one-day shows. However, the climate was different. I couldn't expect such an attentive audience in the real world. Shows had to last longer than one day, but it was financially impossible to stay open round the clock. After a rethink, I came up with Three Day Weekend. The shows/events would occur over a holiday weekend. Three days were the longest time I could spare. The first Three Day Weekend opened on the Ides of March 1994.

When I made studio visits in LA earlier this year I found that the dialogue between artists is stronger than in New York. It actually reminded me of the Glaswegian situation where spaces like Transmission go hand in hand with lots of other artist-run initiatives. In London there has been an explosion of artist-run spaces through the 1990s. What are the similarities or differences in relation to the Life/Live *catalogue?*

In New York there's this thing called "your work." It's separate from your life, and ideally it's nurtured through isolation to keep it pure and strong, denying the discursive possibilities in the formative stages of a practice. I assume that this is done to accentuate and intensify the intrinsically individual qualities that inhabit "the work."

This doesn't occur to the artists in Los Angeles. LA artists play in bands, work as DJs, and put on clubs. It doesn't seem to drain much from their artistic output. On the contrary, more often than not it acts to fuel production. Artistic work is seen as part of a larger latticework of cultural production.

The New York scene sees ideas and concepts as worth something. They're kept like secrets until they've blossomed and are ready to be exhibited. In Los Angeles there still isn't a big art market. There just isn't much to lose. Ideas and concepts are more like discursive elements that flow about between the various loosely defined art factions that make up the LA art scene. The stakes aren't so high here. Artists don't play with their cards so close to their chests. This fosters participation rather than isolation, diversification not specialization.

Unlike most artist-run spaces, your weekends are an irregular activity, they appear and disappear. "Art where we expect it least," as Robert Musil once wrote.

I want to work in an organic manner, to maintain a direct relation between the desire to hold an exhibition and the exhibition itself. I've always entertained the notion that a concept could be proposed for a Three Day Weekend and the show could open the next week. The simple necessities are hard work and publicity.

When I conceived Three Day Weekend I was making a living fabricating things for people. Time and space constraints have always figured into my equation when establishing an exhibition schedule. Three Day Weekend existed primarily in my loft/living space. As my living/studio situations changed, so did the exhibitions.

On the subject of regularity—the only real constant for these shows is a level of intensity, the concentration on putting of a good, interesting show. Interest and concentration have their ebbs and flows. A Three Day Weekend would take place merely because it was time for another show. The irregular exhibition schedule avoids some kind of false consistency, while maintaining an edge that keeps the prospective art audience on their toes. To quote Nauman, "Pay Attention Mother Fuckers."

How do you constitute the artist list for your weekends? It doesn't seem that you follow family curating, as your artists are open at the same time. Is there a continuity in the collaboration with certain artists?

Each exhibition is approached separately. I select artists' practices and arrange the results of these practices in an exhibition. In this way, I see myself as more of an organizer than a curator. I just try to select the most appropriate artists for each project.

Identity production and its considerations weigh heavily here. I'm not too interested in straightforward œuvre production. It's not my job, other people are doing this quite well. I'm particularly interested in artists who respond to varying situations as they see fit: thinking artists who work to solve each particular problem as it arises.

For instance, in graduate school I organized a series of consecutive one-day shows in my studio. I wanted to see if my peers would be willing to work in a more informal or tangential manner than I had seen in their "principle practice"; the shows were successful, surprising in their range and intensity. For four weeks, there was a different show every day. My interests in various artists are piqued through direct interaction. I need to feel a level of comfort with an artist that exists beyond the formal artist-curator situation. In a way, I see my practice as a form of collaboration. The first artists I contacted for shows were friends, but by now the scope has widened. Either that, or I have a lot more friends these days.

The predecessors of these shows are the artist-run spaces of the 1960s; one can even go back further in history and see Courbet's show at the gates of the Universal Exhibition in 1855 as an artist-run show. In LA there was Wallace Berman's Semina, *a handmade Beat literary/art magazine from the late 1950s/early 1960s which acted as an artist-driven magazine, and the Ferrus Gallery established by Walter Hopps and Ed Kienholz in 1957, and so on. In the 1980s these possibilities disappeared.*

LACE [Los Angeles Contemporary Exhibitions] was founded by a group of a dozen or so artists in 1978, but now it's a colossal institution, akin to a small museum. It seems to me that many Los Angeles artist-run spaces are gallery-like, which may well reflect the social climate. For that matter, some LA galleries appear homespun. Food House began as an artists' collective before its directorship narrowed to three people [becoming Acme after relocating to 6150 Wilshire Boulevard in 1998]. Brian Butler ran 1301 out of his apartment. In LA there are always new spaces cropping up. Recently sighted: Ubermain, Spanish Kitchen, 870 Virgil, Lemon Sky, George's, Sin-Du-Da, Room 702, and Post.

One consistent problem with artist-run spaces seems to be conflict between artist's solo career and her/his role as proprietor of the space. Most artists who run spaces see their roles as multiple and separate, and consequently feel a need to choose between them as pressures arise. Thus, as an artist's career takes off he/she may drop the space because it gets in the way. This happened to East Village galleries like International With Monument.

Another factor contributing to attrition is burnout. Running a space does require a great amount of energy. As youthful vigor wanes, many an organizer questions the sanity of killing oneself to put on another show.

Three Day Weekend is run like an artist project. Its collaborative nature is designed to dovetail into my life. I see Three Day Weekend as both a complement to my artistic practice and an integral part of my cultural

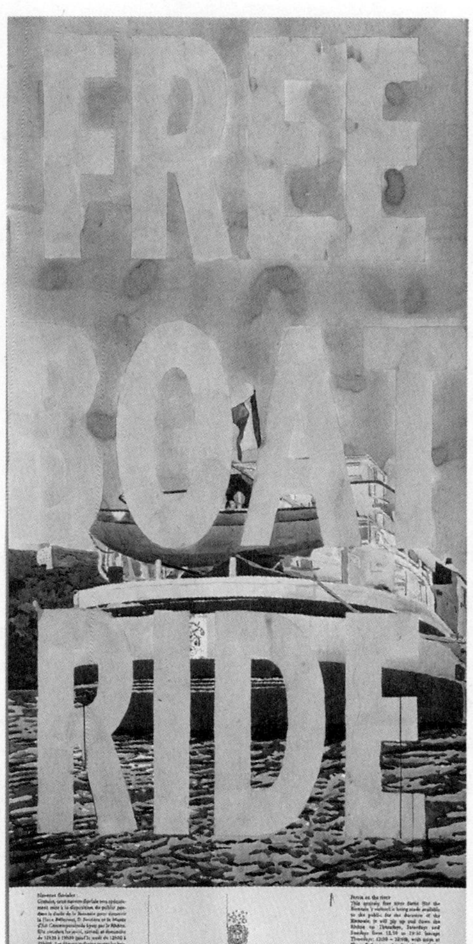

COURTESY OF BLUM & POE | PHOTO: JOSHUA WHITE

Dave Muller
Free Boat Ride, 2004
Acrylic on paper
107 1/2 x 51 inches

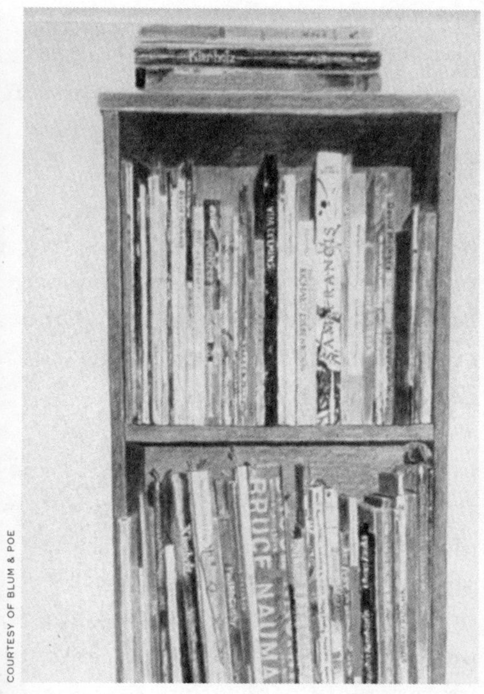

COURTESY OF BLUM & POE

Dave Muller
Rolling, 1998
Acrylic on paper
32 x 40 inches

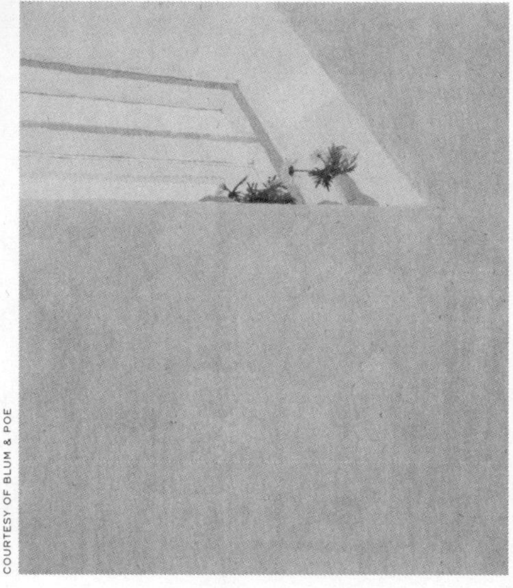

COURTESY OF BLUM & POE

Dave Muller
An Uncommonly Serene Moment, 1998
Acrylic on paper
40 x 32 inches

production. With this in mind, my concept of this artist-run, nomadic project space is malleable enough to change as my needs change. I can see operating Three Day Weekend at any level, as long as I can do them as I see fit. I don't feel the need to choose between my "career" and Three Day Weekend.

What I found striking in LA is that there are not only dialogues among peers but also trans-generational dialogues between artists, for example between Jason Rhoades and Richard Jackson. Does Three Day Weekend consider this, or do you rather see it as platform/tool or your own generation?

In LA it's pretty easy to get to know people, if you want. That's to say that different generations aren't so separate from each other. Many older LA artists teach (which is different from New York) and get to know younger artists through school. The issues that Three Day Weekend might bring up through its sheer existence—the nomadic, DIY, temporality, situational/context, non-monumentality—I see as being topics pertinent to my immediate generation. Obviously, most of these are not new. However, I think their particular combination is.

From the beginning, Three Day Weekend has attempted to cross generations in terms of both participants and audience. I started with my peers. With time this community has diversified, and the median age has gotten older.

As far as dialogues are concerned, do you see the Three Day Weekends as junction makers, in J.G. Ballard's words, triggers of dialogues?

I hope Three Day Weekend works as a trigger on many levels. First, its mere existence should serve as proof that anyone can do this stuff. Secondly, the content of the shows and publications generated should be of enough interest to be considered as cultural production. Thirdly, the openings and related events should have an atmosphere conducive to the direct exchange of ideas throughout the audience. Furthermore, for me to continue, Three Day Weekend must gather enough interest to buoy it from one show to the next. Three Day Weekend's success might be seen as a five-year-long run-on sentence; 30 stops along a sporadic trajectory.

In the 1960s and 1970s the Kunsthalle and a few experimental spaces were places for young artists to go, to hang out, to spend time and to show their work. Today these spaces function like semi-museums. Is Three Day Weekend a reaction to that?

I'm not sure that I am so interested in reacting against anything. Three Day Weekend has always been about creating a sympathetic atmosphere within the confines of my own means. I just want to create something that I don't see enough of in the world.

Your weekends take place either in the exhibition space with the same name in Angelino Heights or they are Gastspiele [hosted] in the context of galleries or museums in other cities. Could you tell me about this oscillation of fixed and floating locations, "both and" instead of "either or" or "nor … nor"?

I feel that Three Day Weekend is a visiting entity anywhere it appears, be it Los Angeles, London, or Houston. Three Day Weekend is designed to occupy a space temporarily. Now this space can be almost any. I've shown videos and played music on chartered bus trips. Last year I set up small shows in two booths at the Chicago Art Fair. When Three Day Weekend takes place in Los Angeles it's usually in my studio. Otherwise, I'm using the studio to make work. Three Day Weekend has the flexibility to work with most any presentable context. I've never considered difficult surroundings a hindrance.

Different contexts each require specific approaches, leading to differing shows. The show that I've put together for the brickwork in Appenzell is not the show I would organize for an old post station in Bern, nor is it the exhibition I staged at Galerie Krinzinger in Vienna. To me, it's impossible to ignore the different contexts of each occasion. Of course, it means more work, but I think this viewpoint is essential. The fact is, a variety of situations is generative as far as I'm concerned. They offer a wealth of stimuli to which I can respond.

Three Day Weekend events are accompanied by handmade printed matter such as small photocopied catalogs and cards. Are these extensions of the show? Do they accompany the show? Is it mail art?

The invitations and catalogs are definitely extended portions of each Three Day Weekend show and are consciously treated as such. Far more people will receive the invitation than will see the show in person. The care that I take in making these small mail pieces reflects that fact. A good card adds to the show, resulting in a more complex relationship between the exhibition and its audience.

The brevity of Three Day Weekend events provides almost an immediate need for something like a catalog. I treat publications as separate from but related to the exhibition. They can be seen as a series of artists' projects in the format of a book. Reproductions of the work in the show are avoided. If people want to see the work they have to see the show; there is no substitute. I'm more interested in including things that elaborate upon an artist's practice. As with exhibitions, I ask participating artists to submit whatever they see fit. Then I'll arrange these submissions into what I think are suitable forms. My aesthetic centers on exploiting innovative possibilities as filtered through an economy of means. I don't find the Xerox format limiting in the least. I just try to make the best publications that I can, within my means.

What role does Three Day Weekend play with regard to your own artwork and music?

Long before I pondered the artistic field I was a college radio DJ. Consider the model of a radio show as it pertains to curating. A successful radio show might be seen as a group of works, arranged and layered in such a manner as to produce meaning that may be different from and greater than the sum of its parts. A good show does this without sacrificing the autonomy of any of the individual pieces. My radio experience grants me a unique attitude toward arranging concepts and objects particularly as applied to notions of authorship.

My approach to arranging work can be seen in the light of improvisational music. It's an evasive topic to write about. The magic of successful improvisation lies in its ability to surprise the listener/viewer with a combination of spontaneity, interactivity, and innovation. How does one practice for this? Utterly unpredictable by nature, this quality can only be recognized. I try to cultivate an awareness that gives me the best chance to apprehend a sense of direction. Apprehension involves a critical approach toward interpretation of experience: a finely tuned grasp of when you are on track.

My current artistic practice arose from the same interests that spurred me to create Three Day Weekend. How is artistic identity established and propagated in the art world? How elastic are the rules governing identity production in this arena? And if these guidelines aren't so steadfast, then why are most attempts at artistic identity production so heavily entrenched in convention? Briefly, I make drawings, and the text that's drawn on them is accurate, as it refers to the location of the show and its dates. The imagery is my conception. I try to render a portrait, not of an artist, but rather of my take on an artist's practice. Three Day Weekend is my foray into cultural production, and these drawings are related interests manifested in the realm of artistic production.

Musical and DJ aesthetics coalesce at Three Day Weekend in a form of ambiance that both uses and has respect for the idiosyncrasies a site has to offer. A trumpet is not a bassoon, but each has its strengths. My musical experience allows for an interestingly odd sense of what might be appropriate, especially when it comes to the interaction of various pieces, either through proximity or content. Hopefully it's like a good radio show: You can hear (see) each separate part, it's all there to be considered, but still the combination of elements makes for something new that can't be reduced to the sum of its parts.

What are your next projects?

A one person show at Three Day Weekend in LA with Anthony Burdin in November, 1998; a Music/Sculpture evening in LA with Solid Eye and various LA sculptors in November or December, 1998. A one-person show with Jory Felice, Elizabeth Saveri, and Jason Middlebrook in the first few months of 1999. Whatever else comes up, I'm game.

* * *

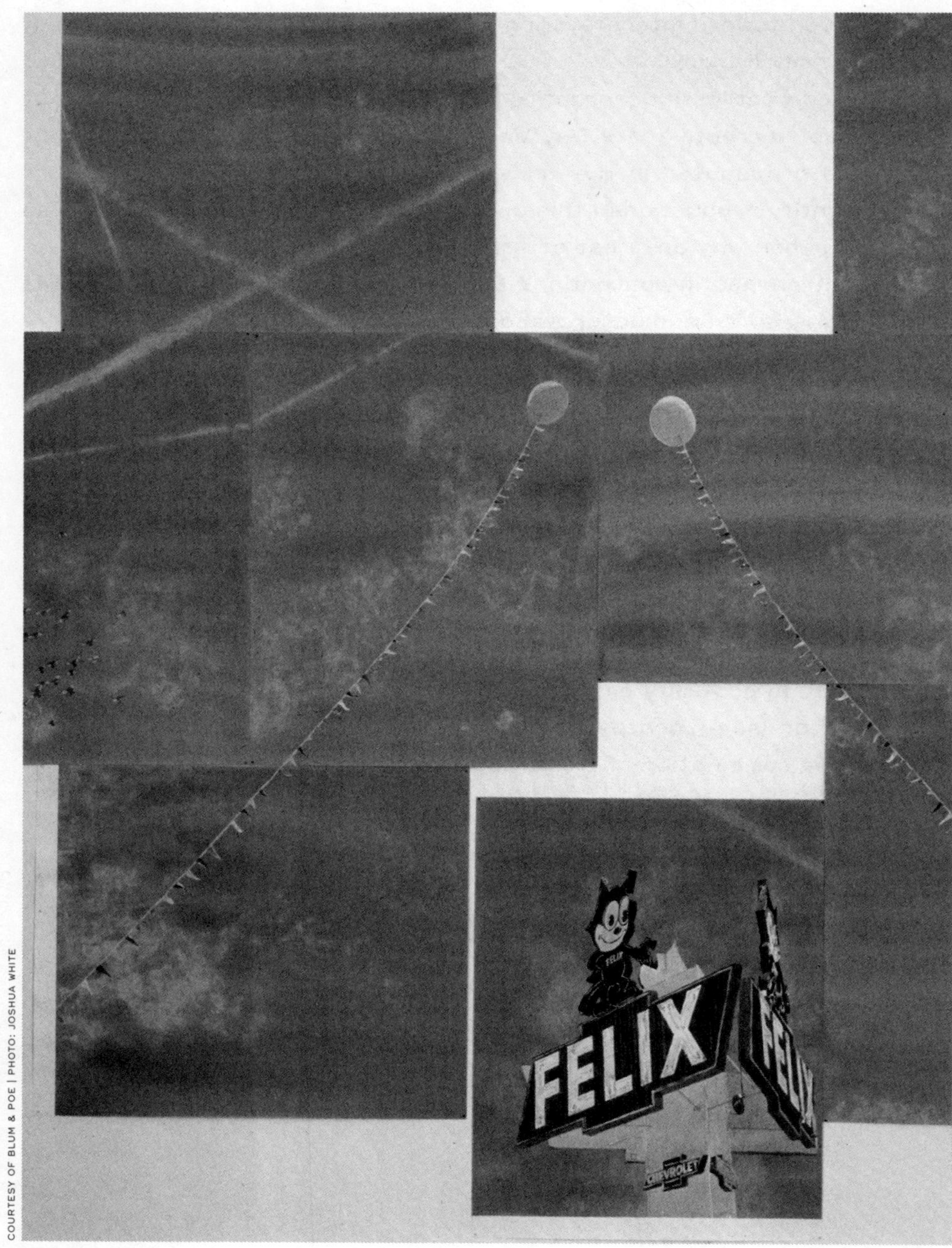

COURTESY OF BLUM & POE | PHOTO: JOSHUA WHITE

Dave Muller
Sprawling (detail), 2003
Installation view from
Blum & Poe, Los Angeles, CA

JOHN WELCHMAN *So, Dave it's 2005 and Three Day Weekend is still going strong—so strong I guess that every time I call you, you're in a different city. When you read over this discussion with Hans-Ulrich, what's changed the most in your approach? Has TDW gone a little mainstream, and if so do you care?*

DAVE MULLER I've actually slowed down the TDW pace a bit. Initially this was because I moved out of a place that had a natural location for exhibitions in October 2001. I would accept the occasional offer to hold a TDW event hosted by other institutions, but now I'm even wary of those offers. Part of TDW's appeal (at least to me) lies in its autonomy. When I work with other institutions, there are decisions about budget, scheduling, and venue that are not exactly left up to me. I didn't initially think that was a problem, but my thoughts changed when the majority (read "all") of the TDW events were hosted. Last year I began to realize that these decisions actually began to form the events more than I felt comfortable with. Perhaps I will feel better when I have another "home venue" to consider as a TDW outlet again. Anyway, the fact that autonomy is an essential ingredient to TDW has been underlined by all this—in fact, more, than I have reckoned with for some time ... Certain institutional banalities threaten my spontaneity.

I got a happily sore neck craning around at the Museum of Modern Art in San Francisco in your one-room show there last year. There was that zony blue, and vapor trails, and palm-tree tips, and the odd 737. It was part wallpaper, part mural, and part muted Tinsel Town kaleidoscope. How has your work on paper developed over the last few years, from your Dave-done-over posters to these dreamily fickle dioramas?

I always thought of the poster-style work as sort of an all-over project, more a view, or a philosophy. I hope that came through in the 2002 Bard/Hammer Museum exhibition, where I thought it important to have over 200 works on view. I felt there was more of a philosophy on display than a collection of separate works.

I began to give myself more authority, perhaps engaging a wider set of interests. While the poster-style drawings had power in their unrequested promotion of and commentary on other artist's practices,

I started to find the premise limiting. I wanted to make work about other things, other interests of mine. This desire became manifest as overall installations of drawings depicting the atmosphere of a night sky or day sky. I think of these groups of drawings as kits, which can be used to outfit an architectural space. Perhaps in this way they are a bit like wallpaper. I think of it as a way to group a large number of my interests (some seemingly contradictory) under a large framework or umbrella.

What have you learned as an artist in the past few years as TDW has attracted institutional-type interests, and your work in galleries has been seen in more museums? It seems to me that there is always, or often, a kind of blind-spot in the career of an artist who begins as an outsider, or who was programmed into alternative or artist-run or independent spaces. Because in one sense you can't quite behave like you did before, you have to modify your work in some way ... or do you? What has happened to some of your peers who didn't go this way, either because they didn't want to, or they weren't chosen?

I don't feel that I've had to change my approach all that much. I mean, I think your approach might be formed out of what you expect from the institution/business of art. And I really did not expect much coming out of school. One thing that I learned from my peers at CalArts was that the really interesting projects did not really even have a framework for discussion yet. They hadn't entered into the art magazine/gallery review/next-cool-thing structure yet.

So I left school wanting to organize shows, and I didn't feel the need to ask any institution to cough up space. I also wanted to make work, but had no idea how my interests might manifest themselves. I liked the autonomy that putting together shows in my own studio allowed. Keeping it financially modest insured that I would have no outside purse strings attached. I organized TDW shows for about a year before I decided that I would learn to draw and make drawings. That interim time was essential. I allowed myself the time to coast, occupying my creative impulses with shows while I could let my ideas for making work click into place.

Coming from a punk-rock background, I'm really not sure what institutions have to offer TDW. I'm even beginning to think that the red tape involved with them outweighs the institutional support structure. For instance, a couple years back I wanted to hold an event where an artist would take a photographic portrait of attendees in their cars. The venue was perfect. There was a parking garage underneath the building, and we could set up an area where you could drive up and get your photo taken. But we couldn't do it because the building was owned by another entity, and they wouldn't allow anything out of the ordinary. I tried all sorts of configurations, which would solve specific problems that the owners were afraid of. No way. And we finally had to come up with something else. So it's that autonomy problem again ...

I've always said that TDW was something that I'd like to do, in one form or another, for the rest of my life. So it's up to me to figure out what I consider sustainable, considering the changes in my life. Maybe these institutional limitations would be less frustrating if I had another outlet. So I'm looking forward to getting a space together in the next year.

What are you working on now, what images are you drawing or painting, what events are you planning?

I'm working mostly in the music milieu. I'm drawing the spines of records from my collection and the collections of others. I'm making wall drawings that depict my ideas for a timeline around the history of music. I'm making drawings that relate the worlds of music to my personal identity.

At this moment I have no TDW events planned ... but I'm always open for discussion.

The Big Squeeze: Micromedia in the Age of Megalomedia

Anne Bray and Holly Willis

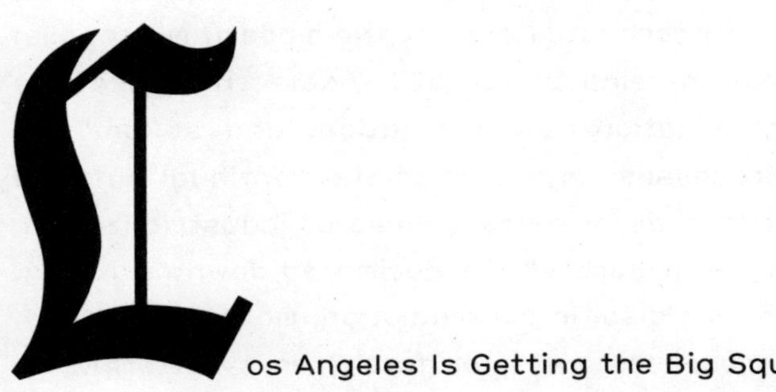

Los Angeles Is Getting the Big Squeeze

It's not new—the open, fecund hand of giving that sprinkled funds across a full spectrum of the independent media scene in the mid-1980s somehow, as if in a very bad dream, morphed into a tight grip of strangulation by the early 1990s. The squeeze forced a shift in media practices, pushing work made in a middle ground of independent production to either the high end of museum-sponsored exhibition and occasional support, with large private institutions unexpectedly (and belatedly) welcoming the dazzling spectacle of moving image art, or to the lower end of ad hoc, guerrilla, and temporary venues as well as low budget, tactical media practices. Media production and exhibition in Los Angeles did not stop as a result of this squeeze; instead, being the incredibly amorphous medium that it is, video art adapted, pushing into new corners for survival as many of the stalwart progenitors of video art and then new media that flourished earlier gasped for breath and finally faded away.

The impetus for the Big Squeeze is complex, and connects on a macro-level with larger industrial shifts faced by the United States and the world as a whole, as well as with specific major events in Los Angeles itself.

First, there is the massive consolidation of media within a handful of transnational corporations. Mergers continue this consolidation today, with fewer than 10 corporations owning more than 90 percent of the world's media.[1]

Secondly, consider what scholar Edward Soja describes as a transformation of the modern city in response to the economic shifts and restructuring that occurred over the last 30 years. In an interview published in *TransUrbanism*, Soja notes, "All aspects of the city are going through a series of what I call de-/re-processes that, taken together, define the deconstruction and reconstruction of the modern metropolis. They include deindustrialization-reindustrialization, deterritorialization-reterritorialization, decentralization-recentralization, and so on."[2] In Los Angeles, the de-/re-processes may refer to the continual outward spread of the city as its edges become new spaces of industrialization, combined with attempts to "reinvigorate" the decimated downtown area. There is movement outward, but also, in contradiction, movement inward. In addition, these de-/re-processes are often furthered by attempts to link them with cultural growth, and indeed, the processes as they appear in LA not only affect media practices, but also describe a series of shifts and reorientations that have altered the media arts landscape several times over.

Third, the fusion of computers and telecommunications and the fact that people are more involved with global networks has also played a tremendous role in the transformation we are attempting to describe, affecting not only artists and the creative potential of new media, but the basic factors of production, distribution, and exhibition. The advent of the Internet and desktop filmmaking meant that artists, curators, distributors, and exhibitors could connect quickly and easily with others around the world, and that people working almost anywhere could network, sharing ideas and contacts. Digital video revolutionized the media-making process, allowing artists to edit and create effects on inexpensive equipment at home; the computer has become a center not only for production, but the site for distribution and exhibition—for the first time, as LA media theorist Peter Lunenfeld points out, artists can use a single machine to make, distribute, and show their work. And concomitantly, the computer has affected the kinds of images that tend to get made.

Fourth, the Culture Wars that rocked the nation also deeply affected Los Angeles. At the heart of this prolonged conflict was an argument over funding—which was exacerbated because the general economy was in recession. But on a deeper level, the issues concerned a shift in the art world itself from modernism to postmodernism, and a pervasive sense that, on the one hand, myths regarding truth and any other foundations had to be dismissed, and on the other, that racism, sexism, imperialism, and homophobia had to be attacked and undermined through art. The ability of artists to deploy politically-motivated art to connect with audiences varied, causing further upheaval, and the overarching result was a decade of tumult: the eruption of several great exhibitions, an amazing body of work perhaps best characterized as issue-based, and the rapid rise and fall of innumerable short-term and temporary spaces.

Fifth, the AIDS epidemic has been painfully significant. While responses to AIDS quickly galvanized the media arts community and resulted in an outpouring of politicized work throughout the US, it took its toll on the Los Angeles media community in that we lost several key curators. Gary Essert and Gary Abrahams, who together created the notorious film festival Filmex in 1971, which they spearheaded until 1986 when the American Film Institute took it over, both died of AIDS in 1991, and their absence was felt deeply. Ken Kirby died on December 27, 1996, after working for close to a decade in Los Angeles. He served as the Director of the American Film Institute's National Video Festival from 1987 to 1990 and then worked as an independent curator for numerous media entities in LA, including LA Freewaves, the UCLA Film and Television Archive, and the Long Beach Museum of Art. More than simply curating, however, Kirby was an outspoken advocate for alternative media practices and for gay and lesbian work. In 1991, he curated a program titled "I, a member" for Freewaves, and in the program notes accompanying the show, he argued eloquently for the maintenance of community in the face of "national jingoism" and "censorial panic," conditions that feel equally worrisome a decade and a half later.

Sixth, there are several very concrete events that have affected Los Angeles over the last 15 years, from the Rodney King verdict to the 1994 earthquake and 9-11. These chaotic events formed the impetus for a growing body of documentary videos that revived the 1970s interest in creating voices to counter mainstream media output.

Finally, there is Los Angeles itself, a sprawling metropolis that for decades was chided for its dispersion and lack of both a shared center and common identity. But the "city without a center" proved to be an apt metaphor for the coming digital age, one founded on Deleuzian rhyzomatic spread. Indeed, if in the mid-1990s Los Angeles was a cheerfully—and abundantly—analog city rife with equipment and artists, socially and culturally it was really a nascently digital city, a cosmopolis already in bits and just waiting for the rest of the world to catch up. The founding of LA Freewaves, a festival of new video and media art held at venues scattered across the city, in 1989 was based on the evolution of the art form, on the shift from analog to digital and on the fact that the city required an entirely new model of dispersed engagement if the media arts were to flourish here.

At the risk of being too reductive, then, we'd like to propose that all of these events and shifts together help weave the backdrop for the development of what we are calling the advent of Los Angeles' micromedia in the age of megalomedia.

The Good Old Days?

In the mid 1980s, Los Angeles, like New York and Boston and other cities in the United States, was enjoying a flowering of alternative media practices. There were numerous strong, active, and well-funded (or well enough funded, since media arts funding has never been abundant) organizations committed to producing and exhibiting new work, and there was a general air of excitement and potential. Among the active organizations were Kaos Network in Leimert Park, the AFI Video Festival, UCLA's Film and Television Archive, Filmforum, VideoLACE, Visual Communication, the Long Beach Museum of Art, and Filmex, all of them in various ways devoted to exploring the power of alternative film and video.

The Long Beach Museum of Art was of particular significance. Its list of illustrious curators includes David Ross, Jackie Kain, Kathy Rae Huffman, Connie Fitzsimons, Michael Nash, and Carole Ann Klonarides, all of whom have been staunch supporters of video and alternative media, both at the museum and beyond it. Indeed, more that any other Southern California institution at the time, LBMA consistently celebrated the work of video artists—shows included work by Bill Viola, Gary Hill, Hilja Keating, Janice Tanaka, Bruce and Norman Yonemoto, Tony Oursler, Mike Kelley, and many others.

In addition to hosting a long list of significant shows, many of which showcased the work of Southern California artists, the museum was also home to the Long Beach Video Annex, a resource that provided artists with editing tools. Finally, LBMA held the largest collection of video art in the United States. Despite the museum's significant position within the arts community, the video programming ended abruptly when then curator Klonarides left in 1995; the museum abandoned media arts and shrunk into provincialism, eschewing its international prominence in the field of video art in favor of being a small-town museum.

If LBMA was—at least temporarily—a strong advocate for video art, it was alone, at least among the major museums in Southern California; in the late 1980s and early 1990s, major museum interest in video art was sparse. Kathy Rae Huffman and Dorine Mignot curated the first show of video art, beyond shows devoted to single artists, at the Los Angeles Museum of Contemporary Art in 1986. Titled *Arts for Television*, the touring show offered a survey of video art by artists. Huffman noted in a conversation with curator Julie Lazar conducted in 2000: "I think it was very timely because it really put the cap on this whole frenzy towards TV ... All these video people were aiming toward TV and it was like this fake dream that just wasn't going to happen. And it was right before the handicam revolution and the whole bottom fell out of funding, and it got changed really fast. The aesthetics changed everything right after that. That was the statement on that era."[3] According to Lazar, who was the founding curator and then Director of Experimental Programs at MOCA, the museum would not host another show devoted to video art until 1998.[4]

The AFI [American Film Institute] was another early supporter of video art in Los Angeles, presenting an annual festival and acting as a central resource for discussions regarding new tools and technological change. However, as with LBMA, interest eventually evaporated, along with funding, which was cut by Sony in 1988, and video artists had to look elsewhere for venues and resources.

Los Angeles Contemporary Exhibitions [LACE] is yet another example, with a strong showing of support and interest in the late 1980s followed by gradual decimation and the loss of financial support. Similar cycles of enthusiasm, presentation, and gradual decline occurred at innumerable other smaller spaces as well. In response, many organizations hunkered down, scaled back and continued on with reduced costs. Despite the tightening grip on funds, however, new entities came to life. In early 1989, Anne Bray, working in collaboration with Ken Kirby, hosted roundtable discussions at the AFI to assess the regional needs for media arts. The conclusion: LA needed a festival devoted to video art that would acknowledge diversity and one that would function pluralistically, working in communication with artists, curators, and members of the community. The first iteration of LA Freewaves' Celebration of Independent Video took place in October that same year. The biennial festival has since shown some 2,500 artists' videos in numerous venues, including museums, billboards, tour buses, galleries, cafés, universities, public TV, and the Web. Freewaves is currently considering television and the Web as outlets and worldwide artists as sources.

Several other organizations attempted to do battle with rather desperate times. Under the leadership of director Jon Stout, for example, the over-20-year-old Filmforum also became more active, continuing the organization's longstanding weekly screenings and programming larger thematic shows. Working in conjunction with The Getty's David Jensen, Stout was able to help rejuvenate the non-profit's flagging finances through a combination of arts funding and corporate sponsorship. In 1994, Filmforum invited several curators, including Tran T. Kim Trang, Thom Andersen, and several of the organization's founders, to help create a program of work charting key moments of alternative media throughout the 20th century. Titled *Scratching the Belly of Beast*, the show was among Filmforum's most ambitious curatorial efforts. Originally founded to support avant-garde filmmaking efforts, Filmforum has made various attempts to include video art in its programming, especially as the boundary dividing film and video has blurred with the advent of digital technology.

If the funding cuts occasioned by the recession were decimating the cultural centers of the city, one response was to try to follow the funding, much of which was re-directed toward youth and related programs. Many arts organizations in Los Angeles created youth educational programs, teaching basic video production and editing to high school students or gearing programming to include the needs of younger audiences.

Yet another response by many artists and curators was to retreat to the protection fostered by an academic environment. Many artists found themselves teaching, and the rich offerings at the city's disparate schools is a testament to the displacement of a once more publicly-oriented art form to the relatively secluded realm of the academy. One of the effects of this has been the evolution of several generations of students steeped in theory and interested in creating essayistic and formally experimental work based on philosophical premises.

What's New?

More recently, LA's academic institutions have been struggling to keep up with the convergence of film, video, design, motion graphics, new media, and gaming, creating hybrid programs that attempt to incorporate several aspects under one aegis. Indeed, with the shift into the academic environment, many video artists turned to new media.

In 1994, Los Angeles was home to the Interactive Media Festival, a showcase of cutting-edge new media projects that not only featured numerous local artists, but also marked a moment of reflection for many people in the city. At that moment, Los Angeles was home to The Voyager Company, which was known primarily for its superior laser-disc releases of international and art-house films, and for the voice-over commentaries leading viewers through the films. However, Voyager was also a pioneer in early CD-ROM technology; the company's Expanded Books were an experiment in creating interactive texts that allowed the "reader" to add to and annotate texts electronically, creating an interactive, potentially nonlinear reading experience. Although The Voyager Company would vacate its beachside Santa Monica office in 1996, the company's presence in LA offered a center of sorts for early discussions of new media; it was also an avid supporter of early interactive works, and released video art collections by Gary Hill and Bill Viola.

Since 1994, Los Angeles has become an extremely active beehive of new media art. The first wave of projects centered on CD-ROM production—Adriene Jenik, for example, who had until that point focused on video art, created a multi-layered adaptation of Nicole Brossard's 1987 novel *Mauve Desert* in 1997, combining moving images, sound, text, and drawings. Christine Tamblyn (1951–1998) was another early innovator in the nascent field, creating two CD-ROMs, *She Loves It, She Loves It Not* (1993) and *Mistaken Identities* (1996), and playing with the properties of the new format. These early experiments suggest that the pleasures of video art—always triumphantly mutable—have shifted to accommodate the creative desires of artists determined to push it into new territory. In this case, video and the computer merged, allowing early experiments of creating within electronic environments. Many of the software programs that are commonplace today were influenced by the desires—and creative demands—of artists who sought to meld and layer image, text, and sound.

Continued new media experimentation in Los Angeles tends to be centered in colleges and universities and includes the creation of challenging works of Internet art, new media installations, and database narratives. Art Center College of Design in Pasadena, for example, was the founding home of Peter Lunenfeld's mediaworks group, established in 1993 and dedicated to fomenting conversation about new media art in its myriad forms. The discussions eventually led to the mediawork Pamphlets, which bring together an artist and thinker to create a text. The series kicked off in 2001 with the publication of Brenda Laurel's *Utopian Entrepreneur*; followed by N. Katherine Hayles' *Writing Machines* (2003), and DJ Spooky's *Rhythm Science* (2004). Each pamphlet is artfully designed to reflect the book's central issues, and each is somewhat experimental in approach, with a mix of autobiography, fiction, and nonfiction in *Writing Machines*, and a fragmented style of *Rhythm Science*.

At the University of Southern California, Marsha Kinder launched The Labyrinth Project in 1997 through the Annenberg Center for Communication. Kinder describes The Labyrinth Project as a think-tank for exploring the potential of interactive narrative. Working with filmmakers and authors, she has overseen the production of several interactive DVD-ROM narrative projects, each of which functions using a database structure.

The number of artists and theorists of new media in SoCCAS schools (including California Institute of the Arts, UC Santa Barbara,

UC San Diego, UCLA and USC) is stunning: Victoria Vesna, Tom Leeser, Erik Loyer, Katherine Hayles, Lev Manovich, Jordan Crandall, Natalie Bookchin, Perry Hoberman, Simon Penny, and George Legrady are only a few of the internationally acclaimed figures in this network working in Southern California. In addition, SIGGRAPH, the annual conference and exhibition held near Los Angeles annually in August, has become a meeting point for artists locally and internationally.

What Does the Art Look Like?

As Kathy Rae Huffman pointed out several years ago, the funding cuts that hit in the early 1990s had a radical impact on aesthetics. Video artists had been almost equally divided between those who wanted to use video as a tool to talk back to established media and those who sought to use it as an extension of other art forms. Numerous LA artists played with the connections and disparities between video art and television—Ilene Segalove, for example, began making videos in 1972, eventually creating a series of rough but endearing personal documentaries about her family in the *Mom Tapes* (1973–1975) and a series of vignettes about the role of television in her life titled *TV Is OK* (1976). Working less in a documentary style and instead playing with the excesses of Hollywood and commercial advertising, LA artists Bruce and Norman Yonemoto, who also began making videos in the 1970s, have often directed their energies toward exposing the manner in which the conventions of television and Hollywood function; rather than offering an alternate to television, they have made many videos that are humorous and/or critical unveilings of the power of media.

On the other hand, there were many artists who saw video as a means to extend—or comment upon—other existing art forms, including sculpture, painting, performance, installation, and even cinema. For them, video's addition of a temporal component made it a privileged form, not only aesthetically but philosophically. Artists in this camp are as varied as Diana Thater, known for her interest in the sculptural properties of a video installation; Jennifer Steinkamp, whose work often concerns the undermining of traditional 3-D space through immersive, large-scale image environments; and Bill Viola, who has used painting and sculpture as reference points in his multi-faceted projects spanning nearly 30 years.

However, cuts in public funding meant that there were few resources for expensive productions or costly sculptural installations, or for projects that did not in some way offer a "return" on the investment. Hence, only a few artists managed to continue working with video in the "high art" vein. The most prevalent form of production that ensued, then, was low budget video making, with an emphasis on tactical media that could be deployed in the service of a political agenda in which the message was more important than its package.

One can see the ramifications of this shift in the kinds of projects produced. Gay and lesbian work flourished, driven by the community's need for artwork that spoke to and about them, as did video art that addressed identity politics in myriad forms. Much of this work was informed by a growing sense that art could be an effective tool in political protest; many students emerging from art and media programs were schooled in poststructuralist theory, and were at once determined to refuse the high art status of Modernism and to use their intellectual resources in media art projects, instead of in traditional essays. The result was the evolution of the essay-based media work, whether in film, video, or new media.

There was also a flurry of confessional work and of projects concerned with shape and experience of memory. This trend was certainly not particular to Los Angeles. Film scholar Andreas Huyssen, surveying a much wider terrain, writes: "The undisputed waning of history and historical consciousness, the lament about political, social, and cultural amnesia, and the various discourses, celebratory or apocalyptic, about *posthistoire* have been accompanied in the past decade and a half by a memory boom of unprecedented proportions."[5] While he is not writing about video art per se, the comment fits this art form perfectly.

Appropriation became a central strategy, too, extending the poststructuralist critique of origins, and by extension, any notion of originality, ownership, and authority. One of its arguments suggested that if advertising and corporate power can use public space to speak to the population, people can take that material, alter it, and offer it back with critique appended. Founded on the idea of the tactic as described by

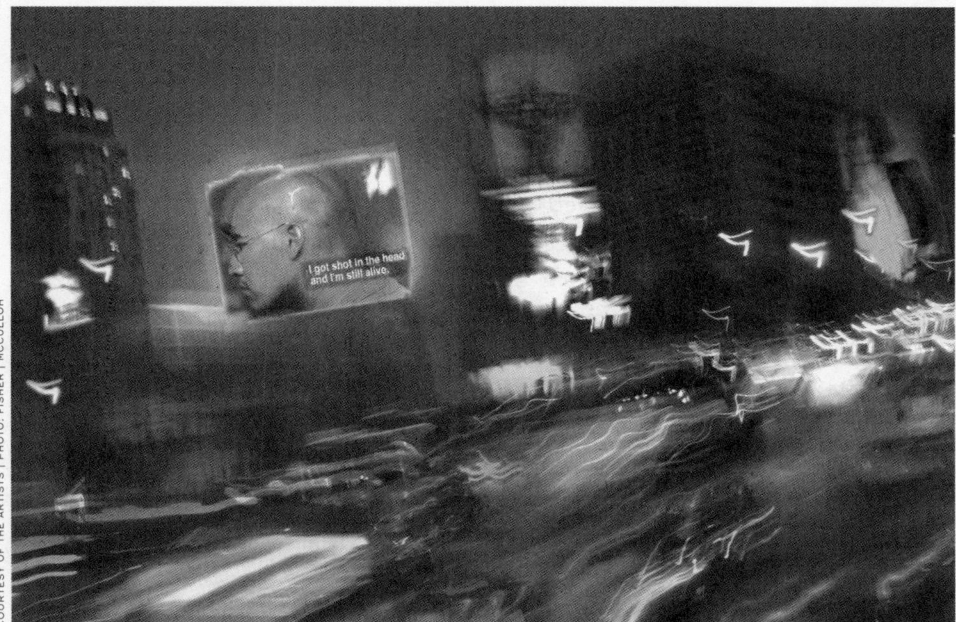

COURTESY OF THE ARTISTS | PHOTO: FISHER | MCCULLOH

Ted Fisher and Douglas McCulloh
20,000 Portraits, 2001–2003
LA Freewaves Video Billboard, Sunset Blvd.

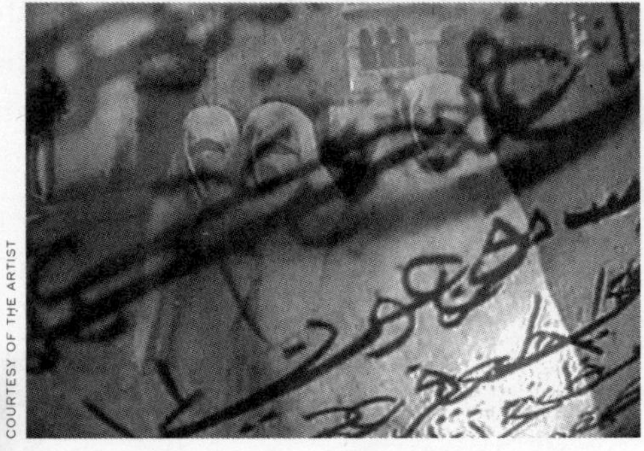

COURTESY OF THE ARTIST

Meena Nanji
Voices of the Morning, 1992
Video, 15 min.

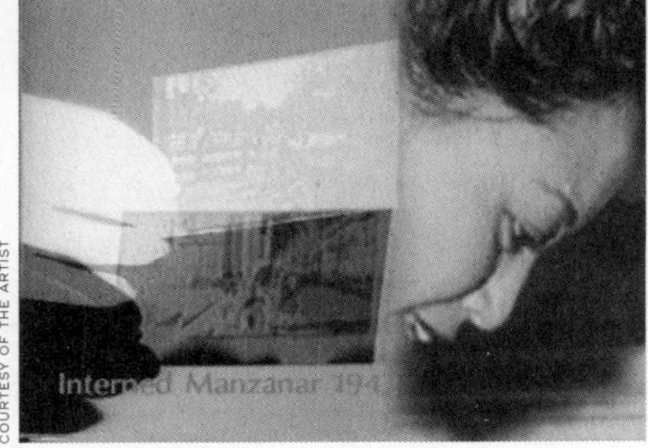

COURTESY OF THE ARTIST

Janice Tanaka
Still from *Memories From the Department of Amnesia*, 1991
Video, 12 min.

theorist Michel de Certeau, appropriation was one tool for fending off hegemonic power by either taking left-overs and detritus and fashioning them into something (despite the lack of public financial support for the arts), or by outright theft.[6] In either case, it is a strategy that does not necessarily cost a lot of money.

Aided by computers, scanners, and the Internet, work based on appropriation continues full force; a striking number of 2004 pre-election artworks have featured re-edited, re-purposed footage of political figures at once hilarious and astounding in their complexity and effectiveness.

As these trends have taken hold, so too has the ubiquity of computer-based production for video and media art. Most media-makers in all genres deal with the computer as the environment within which they work with images. As a result, a shift in emphasis has occurred; artists often spend less time on production, on shooting footage that will then become the foundation for the resulting project. Instead, a project's materials may be a mix of shot material, found footage, stills, text, and sound. Since artists can work on their desktop systems with relatively little cost, more time is spent creating the video during the editing stage, when the core elements can be layered and manipulated for months and even years. As a result, even amateur works are often incredibly complex both visually and aurally.

Thanks to the central role of the computer, which now functions as a staging ground for the material that will constitute the end artwork, the once distinctive differences between film and video have been diminished. Hollywood feature films may still be shot on 35mm, but they are immediately digitized for the post-production process, in which the images are manipulated extensively before being output once again to film. Thus the once decisive line separating (good) film from (bad) video has dissolved. Even the Sundance Film Festival, which for most of its history banned any project shot on video, has gradually gone with the flow, and in 2004 touted its programming of *Tarnation,* a film made on a very low budget using Apple's iMovie.

Paradoxes in the Form of a Conclusion

As we noted earlier, video has proven eminently mutable, adapting to accommodate many disparate demands. But the simultaneous merging of film and video, along with the explosion of video-based interactive, installation, and immersive works is really nothing new. According the historian and critic Rosalind Krauss, we're now experiencing the age of the "post-medium," a term she develops in her extended essay, *A Voyage on the North Sea: Art in the Age of the Post-Medium Condition*:

> Television and video seem Hydra-headed, existing in endlessly diverse forms, spaces, and temporalities for which no single instance seems to provide a formal unity for the whole ... Even if video had a distinct technical support—its own apparatus, so to speak—it occupied a kind of discursive chaos, a heterogeneity of activities that could not be theorized as coherent or conceived of as having something like an essence or unifying core ... It proclaimed the end of medium-specificity. In the age of television, so it broadcast, we inhabit a post-medium condition.[7]

And this brings us to a series of paradoxes by the way of a conclusion. As Krauss notes, video may indeed have no essence or unifying core, but it nevertheless forms the foundation for the increasingly multifarious spread of moving-image-based artworks permeating this region. Further, the oft-touted "democratization" promised first by video and then by digital technology has been glacially slow to arrive—though it is occurring. In 2003, the National Alliance for Media Arts and Culture (NAMAC), and a group of San Francisco-based media arts organizations, partnered with Global Networks to study the future of independent media and concluded, among other things, that the "amount of visual media being created by professionals, committed hobbyists, and amateurs is soaring and will continue to grow for the foreseeable future"; that Internet access will become a standard way for delivering digital media; and that video will "become a fully integrated part of other types of media online ... creating a new demand and uses for video production."[8] The study goes on to highlight the various ways in which video will become increasingly incorporated into everyday life. Thus, as corporate control continues to centralize, creating a massive behemoth, small-scale media art practices continue to push up through the cracks, resisting corporate homogenization. In a sense, then, we're now experiencing a second big squeeze, one occurring from the top down and one which is in turn resisted by counter-movements in and around and through the gaps that inevitably occur.

While the current squeeze repeats those of the past, it's also particular to the conditions of the present. Indeed, our understanding of space and time has shifted dramatically over the last decade, thanks to the growing significance of the Internet in everyday life, globalization, and unprecedented corporate control. We are in the midst of what theorist David Harvey describes as a phase of "time-space compression."[9] Arising at disparate moments in the history of capitalism, these moments of time-space compression "so revolutionize the objective qualities of space and time that we are forced to alter, sometimes in quite radical ways, how we represent the world to ourselves."[10] He goes on to explain that the two goals of capitalist economic activity are centered in space and time—the first attempts to transcend spatial barriers in order to create new markets, while the second is dedicated to increasing the speed of investments and subsequent profit. Time and space seem to become compressed during these phases, a fact that is seen, in turn, in the ways in which we understand, interpret, and represent the world. We have all experienced this compression, both personally and politically, and we see it represented in the media art around us, which reflects on and responds to it both overtly and internally. And once again, even at this macro level, there are small insurgencies, ways of resisting and countering. No matter how big the squeeze, it never quite obliterates what it tries to diminish; instead, things get pinched, pushed, compressed, and distorted, but they ooze elsewhere, finding the overlooked spaces and reappearing, sometimes with renewed energy and invigorated goals.

Notes

1
See media scholar Robert McChesney's book *The Problem of the Media: US Communication Politics in the Twenty-First Century* (New York: Monthly Review Press, 2004) in which the author outlines recent policy changes with regard to the FCC and media ownership. "Whether the United States is approaching a critical juncture with regard to media policy making is yet to be seen," he concludes in his final chapter. "That will depend on the ability of the media reform movement to connect with many other organized political forces in the nation—for example, labor, civil rights, feminism, environmentalism—and draw them deeper into battle." For a helpful illustration depicting media consolidation, see the 2002 diagram in *The Nation*: www.thenation.com/special/bigten.html

2
Edward Soja, in *TransUrbanism* (Amsterdam: V2_Publishing/NAI Publishers, 2002), p. 91.

3
"A Conversation Between Kathy Rae Huffman and Julie Lazar," prompted and transcribed by Sarah Cook, Newcastle upon Tyne, November 30, 2000, for CRUMB (Curatorial Resource for Upstart Media Bliss), available as a PDF online at http://www.newmedia.sunderland.ac.uk/crumb/phase3/nmc_intvw_huffman_lazar.html, p 8.

4
"A Conversation Between Kathy Rae Huffman and Julie Lazar," p. 8.

5
Andreas Huyssen, *Twilight Memories: Marking Time in a Culture of Amnesia* (New York: Routledge, 1995), p. 5.

6
See Michel de Certeau, *The Practice of Everyday Life* (Berkeley: UC Press, 2002).

7
Rosalind Krauss, *A Voyage on the North Sea: Art in the Age of the Post-Medium Condition* (London: Thames & Hudson, 1991), p. 31.

8
http://www.namac.org/article.cfm?id=344

9
David Harvey, *The Condition of Postmodernity: An Enquiry Into the Origins of Cultural Change* (Oxford: Blackwell, 1990), p. 240.

10
Harvey, p. 240.

Strangeways Here We Come

Rita Gonzalez

> If we make art, as though we know what's going to happen, whether it is hopeful or cynical, we're not working on an art project—we're working *against* an art project! Only with great uncertainty can some, very small achievements be made for some future that we cannot see or imagine. We have to work in strange ways and hopeless ways but not cynical ways.
> – Jimmie Durham[1]

I empathize with Jimmie Durham's exhaustion and optimism. Looking back to engage with a recent past demands certainty, but you might consider my current undertaking as pretext to an unforeseen future. I was dislocated from Los Angeles, my lifelong home, for a number of years. Throughout the 1990s I lived in Northern and Southern California. Yet I never quite left LA. This intervallic essay reflects my tuning into the recent past and is culled from dialogue, research, and remembrance.[2]

Toward a Development of the "Conceptually Political"

Two young art students discover one another while perusing the stacks of a college library. Unlike a clichéd movie moment, they don't bump into each other literally, but slowly come to recognize the other's imprint in the rubber date stamps of two particular library books. The books in question: catalogues for *Helter Skelter: LA Art in the 1990s* (Museum of Contemporary Art, Los Angeles, 1992) and *Chicano Art: Resistance and Affirmation [CARA]* (UCLA Wight Gallery, 1990). The artists' meeting takes place a few years after these exhibitions and, significantly, in the aftermath of the Los Angeles uprising.

For them, these two books, *Helter Skelter* and *CARA*, replayed a moment in the city when the focus was on repairing civic discontent, dealing not only with racism in black and white but also as it had erupted across racial, ethnic, and class lines.

These benchmark exhibitions mattered in wildly different ways, yet provided certain conceptual underpinnings for an emerging group of artists in the 1990s. While *CARA* was an exhibition organized according to the pedagogy of consensual politics (with a strong concern for establishing the socio-political climate for Chicano art production), *Helter Skelter*'s lone curator, Paul Schimmel, produced a dark counter-narrative to the received ideas of Los Angeles in both popular culture and art history.[3] Furthermore, Schimmel's exhibition fueled the "LA effect" in contemporary art discourse, propelling it in another direction. *CARA* was a show predicated on ethnic specificity and the ongoing reckoning of art and politics. *Helter Skelter* presented artists and writers of color in both the exhibition and cataloge—yet probably for the first time since the height of multiculturalism, artists' identities did not result in either a label or a cordoned-off section reserved for *difference*. What the two library-dwelling art students *did* notice was that the artists and writers of color included in *Helter Skelter* did not produce content that was illustrative of what had become by the early 1990s an acceptable ethnic aesthetic. They also noticed that some of the most dissonant and complex work associated with *CARA* came through the academics, critics, and artist/theorists who contributed to the cataloge, rather than the exhibition itself.

Harry Gamboa Jr. served as interlocutor for both exhibitions, appearing in *CARA* as artist and writer, and as fiction writer in the *Helter Skelter* cataloge. Gamboa's images and writing were in dialogue with his notion of phantom identities—identities considered marginal to institutional and cultural arbiters of meaning, taste, and relevance.[4] Gamboa's assertive casting of phantom identity had a sympathetic connection to identity-based claims for "resistance and affirmation," but rather than championing the uplifting images and words of the folkloric, the communal, or the ethno-national, Gamboa chose the urban, the discordant, and the stateless. Gamboa describes the divide between some of the university-trained artists who "consciously portrayed the various elements of contemporary Chicano culture that dealt with the obvious symbols of material identification, i.e., lowrider automobiles, tortillas, tattoos, traditional ceremonies, and modified graffiti,"[5] and those "urban realists" and barrio existentialists with whom he identified. Gamboa insisted on theorizing the "phantom culture" in an attempt to document the simultaneous experience of being hyper-visible—in the repertoire of ethnic stereotypes—and invisible—on an institutional level. Asco ("nausea" in Spanish, 1971–1987), the conceptual art group with which he first began to produce as an artist, was not guided by an overriding ideology but, in Gamboa's words, by "conceptually political" strategies.[6]

So how did the shows resonate for the two art students? And how did the collision of each show's sensibility play out in their work? Ultimately, Mario Ybarra Jr. and Ruben Ochoa (the two mystery art students) would spend the latter part of the 1990s making work derived from a radical juxtaposition of the consensual politics of *CARA* and the crypto-political, aesthetically violent material of *Helter Skelter*. Ybarra Jr. would create monstrous hybrids culled from a wild-style mixture of urban subculture and the Babel-like noise of clashing immigrant outposts of Los Angeles. Ochoa would rip the zoot suit out of time, fashion a new one from shards of broken glass, and wear it in a performance at a museum exhibition opening for Dale Chihuly's glass sculptures.[7] His raucous entrance caused severe panic.

Post-*Helter Skelter* and the Rise of the MFA in Los Angeles

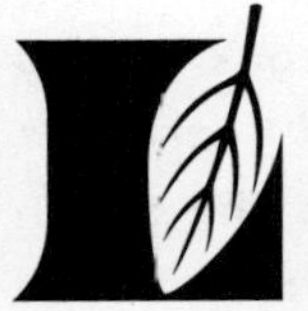*AX: The Los Angeles Exhibition 1992* developed in the shadows of MOCA's *Helter Skelter*. Staged around Los Angeles in seven different alternative artist spaces and cultural centers,[8] its multiple shows represented various outpost identities of artists living in Los Angeles, as well as the alternative spaces in which they most often performed and exhibited. As Los Angeles art and art schools gained notoriety during the late 1990s, a number of the spaces included in *LAX* would fold or radically change their agendas. The profiling of the Los Angeles art scene would soon shift to both popular and scholarly mappings of its graduate-school offerings.[9] As the issue of pedagogy, and the rise of the LA art schools are so crucial to the evolution of the

Southern California art scene, here's a longish excerpt from a series of exchanges between *LAX* organizer Ed Leffingwell, artist Fred Fehlau, and writer Amy Gerstler. In response to a discussion of exclusionary tactics in Los Angeles art spaces, Fehlau states:

> ... it must also be said that there are many involved in this argument (ethnic-specific institutions included) that have done as much to maintain these differences as the powers that be. In a draft of an essay for this cataloge, Plaza de la Raza defined its mission as an effort "to continue to offer Chicano, Mexicano, and Latino artists an opportunity to add their voices and perspectives to the discourse of contemporary art." The text refers to the fact that although Frank Romero, the subject of the Plaza's exhibition for "LAX," has exhibited extensively throughout the world, he has never had a solo exhibition within the community ("his community") that inspired his greatest works. In this context, the drawing back of one of our "own" further defines Romero and his work as a direct expression of an individual community. Chevy "lowriders" and East Los Angeles landscapes become illustrations of an experience, or in other terms, an expression of "lifestyle." In that, they remain the property of that particular group, effectively secluded and removed from the community of ideas and individuals at large.
>
> As an aside, I must relate a classroom experience I had a few years ago. A student presented a series of images based upon a historical and cultural narrative of cockfighting in the rural Black South. That same month, *Angel Heart* was playing in local movie theaters, a film also set in the South and including scenes of cockfighting and religious rituals and sacrifice. The images in the student's work were grainy and rough, and certainly had the double-edged look of fashion and documentary. But the reality was that the student, who is African-American, got a bunch of her friends together, all of whom live in Los Angeles, and in true Hollywood fashion 'staged' the event, complete with poultry and sexual overtones. The student had no direct experience with that ritual

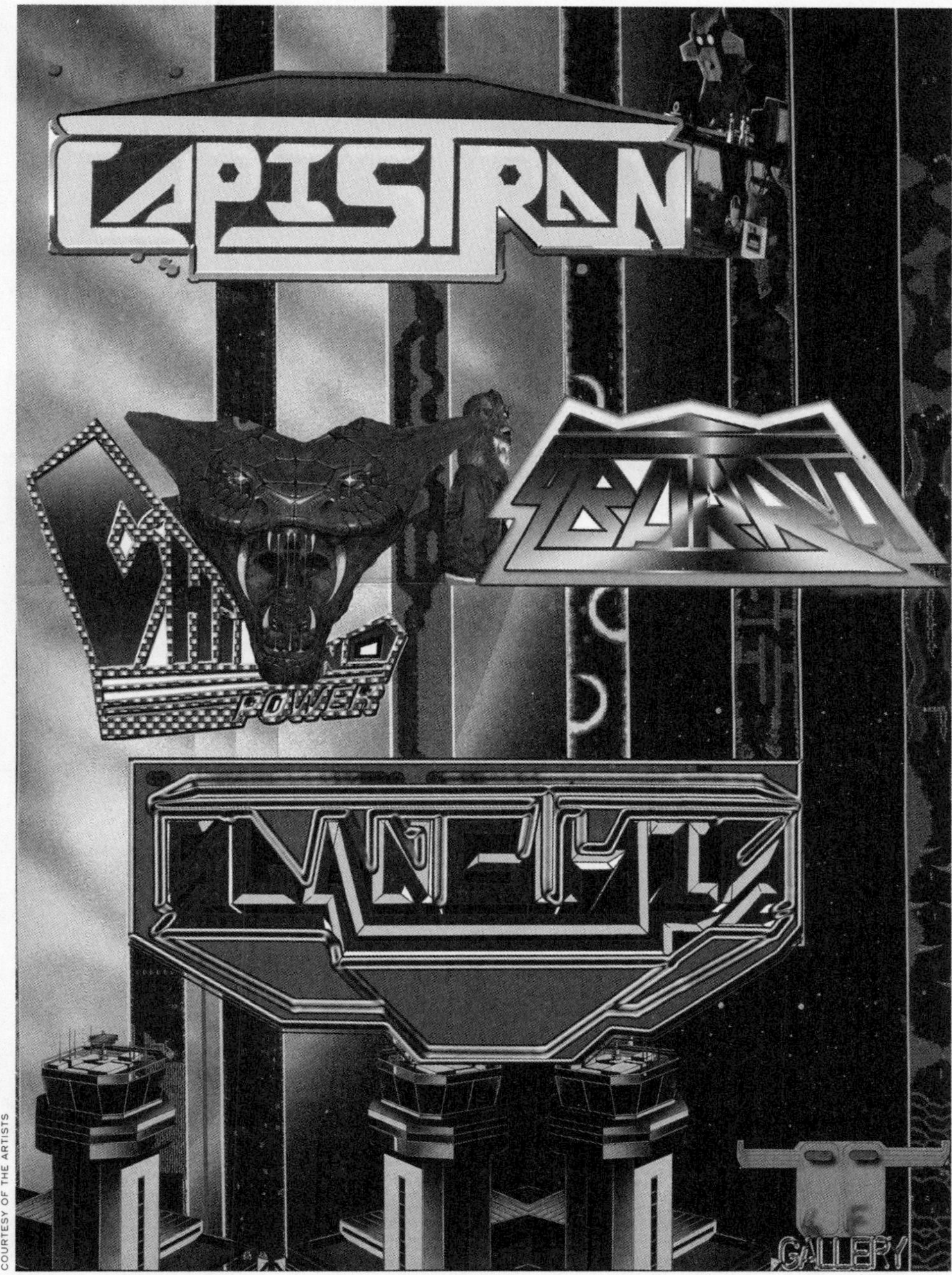

COURTESY OF THE ARTISTS

Slanguage (Mario Ybarra Jr. and Juan Capistran)
Sonido Slang, 2003
Light jet print, 30 x 40 inches

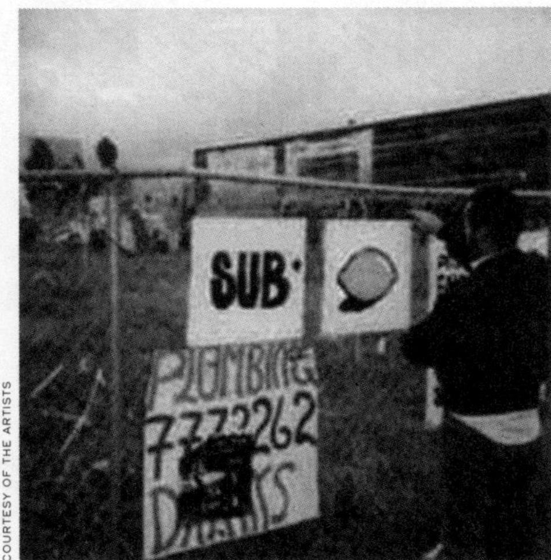

COURTESY OF THE ARTISTS

Slanguage
(Mario Ybarra Jr. and Juan Capistran)
Sublime, 1998
Documentation of hand-painted posters installed in South Central Los Angeles

> and, upon discussion, could not find any reason why she, as a Black woman, would necessarily be more informed of or familiar with these images than anyone else in the classroom. The reason, of course, was that all of our readings (of the piece, the representations, and the ritual) were constructed from a shared and mediated set of information, information that was intended to be and produced to be *familiar*. Although everyone recognized the story, no one could recognize themselves in the story. An opposite but corollary point can be made about Frank Romero's work: while most everyone can recognize and understand the imagery (whatever stereotypes and generalizations that maintains is another issue), the author's assumption is that the audience at Plaza de la Raza will be able *to identify themselves through it*.[10]

I read over Fehlau's comments several times; and although he, Gerstler, and Leffingwell were involved in a fast-paced exchange of gut responses and anecdotes and did not, perhaps, conceptualize their text with the rigor of a critical essay, a certain poignancy in it rang true for me. After many discussions with artists who went through MFA programs from the 1990s through the early 2000s, I find in Fehlau's text a crystallization of several important "post-MFA" issues, most notably, mentorship, authenticity, and reception. Fehlau's classic liberal response to his student indicates some of the continuing complexities that art students face in critiques. Emerging artists, especially in the Los Angeles art schools, are often given wildly divergent opinions about cultural aesthetics, identity politics, and community accountability.

Reading Howard Singerman's book *Art Subjects: Making Artists in the American University* recently, I was struck by his comments on the determinations of political art's critical success. Singerman notes that while most proponents of political art are outwardly concerned with the relevance of what they do to a particular community, the significance of their practice and the discourse it generates is ultimately appraised by academia. As Singerman goes on to note, this "doubledness of political art" does not necessarily short-circuit its political capacities; but it does broach a range of issues alluded to in Fehlau's address, particularly the idea that what comes from a politically-oriented and community-bound practice runs the risk of serving as “a report for outsiders on an authentic inside.”[11] Contemporary artists renounce authenticity claims because of the numerous forces that affect their art practice. Didactic and illustrative tactics are complicated by trans-cultural or subcultural allusions and by an unmooring of an instantly recognizable ethnic or racial aesthetic.

The growth in the numbers of artists of color who are receiving MFAs (or who study with mentors of color) has had a direct impact on the proliferation of attitudes about protectionism, community accountability, and professionalization. Those who share the concerns of the writer of La Plaza de la Raza’s entry (referenced by Fehlau) still maintain the necessity of cultural specificity and a space of their own. However, there are those shaped by spaces such as La Plaza de la Raza (est. 1970) and Self-Help Graphics (est. 1973) who understand the continuing need for activism and education, but are also critical of separatism and protectionism.

Collisions

About a decade before Ybarra and Ochoa’s chance meeting, another collision of attitude occurred somewhere in downtown Los Angeles. Reflecting on his initial encounter with Harry Gamboa, artist Daniel J. Martinez remarked, “Harry was the first Mexican-American I met who was like me. We are both light skinned and not exactly stereotypically Latino in our looks. He didn’t speak Spanish. He didn’t do murals. He was interested in language. He was interested in conceptual art. We started to talk about identity, politics, and we talked about a new, reinterpreted version of conceptual art.”[12] What is key for my own account of LA art in the 1990s is not only the artistic output of Gamboa, Asco, and Martinez, but the curious manner in which the metal shards that make up Gamboa’s language and the grenade-like sentences fired off by Martinez have been responsible for the development of several artists and critics who emerged in the 1990s. Although Gamboa and Martinez stopped conversing and collaborating back in the late 1980s, each has been called upon for public forums and both have made their marks as educators throughout Southern California.

Although I do not have the space in this essay to discuss the artistic and discursive output of Gamboa and Martinez in the detail they merit, I will say that, simply put, drastic changes have occurred in the rendering of the "conceptually political strategies" of an emerging group of artists and scholars because of Gamboa's and Martinez's artistic and discursive example.[13] But I want to move on to consider the work of a generation of artists in their late 20s and early 30s that illustrates various "conceptually political strategies" in its engagement with language, history, and depictions of urban space as strange fiction. The following artists concoct counter-memories in part to derail expectations (of what art by a Chicano/Mexican-American should look like), and in part to betoken things to come.

The Pocho Research Society

Underscoring the invisibility of multiple histories of Los Angeles, *Operation Invisible Monument* (2002) and the recent *October Surprise* (2004) are projects of the Pocho Research Society of Erased and Invisible History (PRS), an organization that operates in secrecy but is known to work with visual artist Sandra de la Loza. In their founding statement, the PRS claims to understand "history as a battleground of the present, a location where hidden and forgotten selves hijack and disrupt the oppression of our moment."[14] The PRS layers the discourse of clandestine militant action with the benign gestures of historical memorializing—not simply to produce a subtle insertion into a landscape, but to generate debate on the use and rendering of sites and entire communities.

The PRS uses the historical plaque, an often subtle sign affixed or adjacent to a building or architectural domain, in order to camouflage its radical intentions. By blending into asphalt and brick, these faux monuments perfectly simulate the gravitas of the historical marker. The language employed by PRS also mimics the elegiac tenor of the sanctioned civic plaque. In *Invisible Monument #4*, a graffiti artist named Chaka is given a marker titled "Triumph of the Tagger." The text reads:

> During the late 1980s an invisible army assaulted the city with spray cans transforming bland concrete walls into canvases filled with an explosive language of hard-edged urban forms, radiating color, and an abstract coded lexicon. The most prolific, the Boyle Heights tagger known as Chaka, single-handedly inflicted $30,000 worth of damage [on] the Southern Pacific Railroad.

While PRS enshrines subversive figures and spaces (among those it celebrates are a short lived punk club called the Vex and DeCenter, a post-LA uprising resource center run by local anarchists), the organization also selects sites that have been the center of revisionist historical debate on both the scholarly and community level. In PRS' series *Operation Invisible Monument*, operatives placed a surrogate monument alongside one paying tribute to the site of Dodger's Stadium. The PRS monument narrated the displacement of the inhabitants of Chávez Ravine, a community of mostly Mexican-American families that existed in Solano Canyon until the development of Dodger Stadium.[15]

It is important that the historical plaques are installed clandestinely, usually under the cover of darkness, and without the permission of public officials; and are then immediately documented. The resultant 'landmarks' ultimately exist only as documentary evidence of a performance perpetrated in isolation, since security guards or property owners consistently remove the plaques shortly after their installation. The blanket disapproval of PRS' monuments evidenced by their speedy removal, suggests that these types of sites "await the development of interpretive traditions within which they can be assessed, framed, and promoted."[16] While most monuments are designated for sanctioned spaces and designed to impart a condensed lesson about a landmark event or key facilitator in civil society, the "counter-monuments" of the PRS operate in the erased spaces of community memory to champion the forgotten subjects of history. PRS is keenly aware that the graphics they produce for insertion in notionally public spaces (but actually private property) are counter-memorials. That is, the plaques emblematize the constant threat of the evaporation of cultural memory in relation to what gets documented—and memorialized—by official historical discourse.

The Slanguage Sublime

In addition to meeting Ruben Ochoa at Otis College of Art and Design, Ybarra Jr. also came into contact with Juan Capistran. They started collaborating shortly after the Los Angeles uprising of 1992, in part because of their shared interest in public uses of urban space after the riots. Capistran was born in Mexico but his family settled in South Central Los Angeles when he was a child. Ybarra was raised in Wilmington, the harbor area of Los Angeles. Both have mentioned that growing up outside East Los Angeles (generally considered the Southern California center of Chicano political and cultural identity) shaped their notions of self in relation to urban identities, allowing them to be more aware and in synch with multiple subcultures and ethnicities.[17]

I call their work tactical graphics. Tactical graphics mine and mimic the designs and distribution networks of the informal economies and underground cultural and sub-cultural events that occur throughout Los Angeles (or any other city with a constantly changing demographic). Tactical graphic artists add another layer to the urban palimpsest and intervene in sites that are under erasure. They are feedback generators, recycling the visual and aural noise that for the most part goes unnoticed by those who do not listen to Spanish or Vietnamese language radio shows; or for those who do not shop at predominantly Latino or African American small businesses; or for those who do not attend Chicano punk shows.

After the riots, many buildings, especially in South Central and Korea Town, lay in ruins. Chain link fences went up on major boulevards and individuals started to use these fences as bulletin boards to post ads for their unique services (braiding, plumbing, car repair, etc). Ybarra and Capistran were attracted to these handmade signs and intervened with their own series of *Sublime* paintings. Their hand-painted signs were placed amidst the other homemade signage on corners throughout South Central.

Since then Ybarra and Capistran have created work and performed under a number of handles (Space Invaders 13 and AllModCons, among others). In 2002, Juan and Mario opened an alternative space called Slanguage, a combination studio, site for guerrilla education, and exhibition

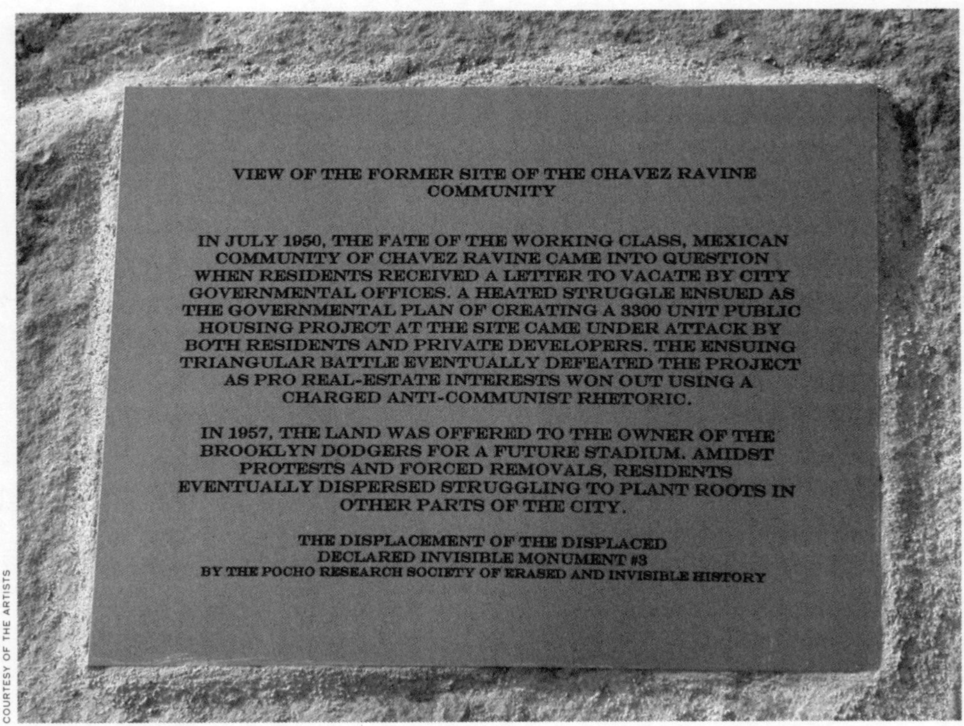

COURTESY OF THE ARTISTS

Pocho Research Society of Erased and Invisible History
Operation Invisible Monument, 2002
Documentation

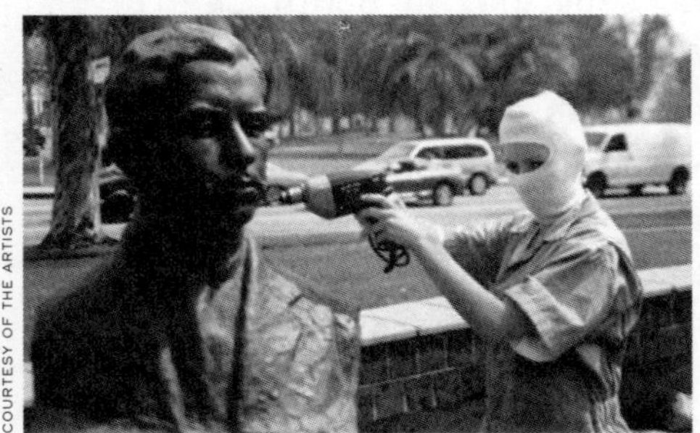

COURTESY OF THE ARTISTS

Pocho Research Society of Erased and Invisible History
Operation Invisible Monument, 2002
Documentation

space. The neologism "slanguage" suggests a mutation of common speech—a street-level transfusion. This new formation is born out of an aural and pictorial sensitivity to noise. Ybarra and Capistran translate and generate street-level articulations (of mixed [up] identity, of urban sampling, of altered forms of popular culture), and as such, both artists function as the lexicographers of this new Slanguage.

One facet of Slanguage has been the visual language of black-market promotion vis-à-vis tactical graphics. The poster diptych *Sonido Slang* (both 2003) uses a digital output to simulate a popular graphic design style popular in the promotion of *banda* and *norteño* acts in Southern California. Ybarra and Capistran were drawn to the fonts and designs used in these posters, especially in relation to an influential Japanese science fiction aesthetic that would seem to run counter to the aesthetics of *narcocorrido*. As hip-hop culture has taught Ybarra and Capistran, a new language and visual code is necessary for the creation of alternative educational and cultural production models.

Imaginary Murals and the 21st Century

After strolling through the 18th arrondissement, Scoli Acosta is distracted with thoughts about the murals of Los Angeles. He is 5,673 miles from the city but starts a drawing anyway. He titles it *The Imaginary Mural of Los Angeles*. Like old cartographies that miniaturize the city and bloat the hand of the draughtsman, the corner of his drawing features a gaunt, disembodied hand in the process of mapping. The washed-out colors reprise those faint hues long familiar to Thomas Guide devotees. However, users of such guidance devices would run pell-mell from Acosta's labyrinthine map.

Acosta attended Los Angeles County High School for the Arts (LACHSA) located at the brutal (yet aerially sublime) intersection of four urban freeways. The divisiveness of the freeway—and its harsh ramifications for the mostly Mexican/Chicano population—gave birth to a series of epic projections on the public-facing walls of stores, libraries, housing projects, and cultural centers. Acosta grew up with these and with other daily transformations of his urban surroundings. Punks, beatniks, neo-Aztecs, Mexican rockeros, Beverly Hills nannies, and former Jetters crossed his path. His uncle Sean Carrillo was a participant in the expanded line-up of Asco in the 1980s. In the 1990s, Acosta would get an MFA at the Kansas City Art Institute, followed by years of travel through Europe. His extended foray involved the building of an elaborate archive (composed out of hand-crafted and found artifacts) devoted to his double passion for French 19th century writer Gérard de Nerval and documentation of his own intermittent performances.

Why does this 21st century nomad, this suburban refugee who grew up on the nectar of Los Angeles river water, beat culture, and sonic confusion, make work that looks and sounds like it is from another dimension of time and space? *The Imaginary Mural of Los Angeles* is what one sees projected across time after walking through Paris on an extended lark. It is a dim and unruly memory shaped in a city overloaded with history—about a mega-city that regularly recycles its own. *The Imaginary Mural* has no boundaries—just endless contortions like the unpredictable flow of LA River water. The map flows out of the black veins of a floating hand that hovers over the city like a phantom.

Thelma Golden and Glenn Ligon set off the Post-Black Effect, or; *If Post-Black is the new Black ... then what is the new Brown*?

We gathered together—some fifteen artists, art historians, and curators—at a round table to discuss the state of contemporary art, or rather (echoing one of the participants) whether or not we *matter* to the state of contemporary art. All of those gathered were "Latino" but we used Chicano art and its newly historical status as a starting point for our comments. The topic "post or wave" (conceived by artist/writer Ken Gonzales-Day and myself) was meant—one way or another—to differentiate us from an artistic culture that served as an auxiliary of a political movement.[18] Were we "post-Chicano"—a term actually concocted by art critic Max Benavidez in the early 1990s[19]—or were we—on the model of second and third wave feminism—in a historiographic mode characterized by empathy, respect and distance? Or were we seeking an exit strategy from all of the above?

Although this roundtable took place in 2004, our dialogue was a sort of summary judgment of the last two decades in which most of us were educated and acculturated. We had all taken different paths—some were the daughters and sons of activists in *el movimiento*, others were the descendents of Central Americans affected by US interventions. Culturally, we were shaped by anything from hip-hop to Sub Pop, from Morrissey to Queer Nation—from the art of political graphics to Minimalism. We were there around the table—we were impressed, we were supportive, we were scheming—and we ended up turning *against* definition. Ultimately, our group epiphany arrived at a mutual dissatisfaction with any staple term or seamless category. Of course, some of us felt more attuned to "strategic ambivalence," while others had worked out a way of dealing with our perceived irrelevance through any number of canny tactics. As curator and art historian Ondine Chavoya pointed out, the artists that interested and inspired him were those engaged in "situations not institutions." Many at the table acknowledged similar penchants: strategies for survival in the art world and avoidance of historical myopia. But each participant had a different way of adjudicating her or his position.

One artist at the table suggested that we could no longer be impractical in our dealings with the art world—that if we continued with the same cycle of self-examination, we would continue to be irrelevant. He called the framework for our roundtable "repeating lyrics on a broken CD." And he was surely right. Since the onset of conversations about an ethnically specific aesthetic practice in the early 1970s, there has always been a false dichotomy between art world success and an isolationist notion of authenticity. The frustrated artist went on to cite the 9/11 Commission's findings that the cabinet of George W. Bush suffered from a "failure of imagination"—and made the connection to our very own critical meltdown. Although I agreed with the urgent call for an imaginative expansion of our art production and critical work, I did not think we could ignore the disparities and inconsistencies that still drive art world institutional and discursive practices.

Some left the meeting rather weary, with a sense that recent MFAs want to distance themselves from identity politics altogether. Artists Christina Fernandez and Sandra de la Loza voiced discontent with an amnesiac strain in the discussion, suggesting the critical importance of the Chicano and feminist movements. We agreed on one thing, at least, that without a doubt the terms Chicano/post-Chicano should cease to be the sole generators of (and refuges from) curatorial and critical paradigms. Earlier generations of artists were beset with the same semantic dilemmas; so it seemed clear that, at the risk of stagnation, the group should discuss the issues and processes that drive their work, and, in doing so, search for areas of critical intersection and mutual relevance. What seemed utterly clear was the fact that manifestations of dissent and agitation from the late 1960s to the present had laid the groundwork for upcoming generations to have the liberty to choose when, where, and how to deal with the contextualization of identity in their work. But what also seemed clear was that the drive of artists to be "known by their art" was also based on a romanticized notion of the artist operating in the fluffy drift of formal purity.

We have to work in strange ways and hopeless ways but not cynical ways.

Notes

1
Jimmie Durham, “Probably This Will Not Work,” *Strategies for Survival—Now! A Global Perspective on Ethnicity, Body, and Breakdown of Artistic Systems*, ed. Christian Chambert (Lund, The Swedish Art Critics Association Press, 1995), p. 223–235.

2
In particular, I would like to acknowledge the following friends and colleagues who shared many insights: Sandra de la Loza, Ondine Chavoya, Ken Gonzales-Day, Daniel J. Martinez, Jim Mendiola, Mario Ybarra Jr., Jennifer Sternad-Flores, Juan Capistran, Bill Kelley, Ruben Ochoa, Perry Vasquez, Ruben Ortiz-Torres, Yanira Cartageña, and Pete Galindo. I would also like to thank John C. Welchman, Ondine Chavoya, and Joseph Mosconi for their invaluable editorial assistance.

3
For an examination of the influence of Lynn Foulkes and Robert Williams as the senior emissaries of “dirty pop” in the Los Angeles art scene, see Howard Singerman on “Helter Skelter,” *Artforum* vol. XLIII, no. 2 (October 2004), p. 125–126, 284–285.

4
For a primer to Gamboa’s oeuvre, see Chon Noriega’s “No Introduction,” *Harry Gamboa Jr. Urban Exile: Collected Writings of Harry Gamboa Jr.*, ed. Chon Noriega (Minneapolis and London: University of Minnesota Press, 1998), p. 1–22.

5
Harry Gamboa, “Serpents in the City of Angels,” *Artweek*, 20, 1989, p. 24.

6
C. Ondine Chavoya has treated the spatial productions of Asco in “Orphans of Modernism: the Performance Art of Asco,” in *Corpus Delecti: Performance Art of the Americas*, ed. Coco Fusco (London & New York: Routledge, 2000), p. 240–263.

7
Ochoa executed this performance at the opening for “Chihuly: The George R. Stroemple Collection” at the California Center for the Arts, Escondido, in 1999. For his account of the performance, see Ruben Ochoa, “Breaking Down Glass Walls,” *Aztlán*, vol. 28, no. 1 (Spring 2003), p. 175–178.

8
The exhibition was coordinated by Ed Leffingwell of the Municipal Art Gallery in Barnsdall Park, and included a general survey at the Barnsdall Park gallery; installations at the Fisher Gallery at the University of Southern California and the Santa Monica Museum of Art; abstract art at Otis School of Art and Design; two crafts artists at the Japanese-American Cultural Center; a retrospective of painter Frank Romero at the Plaza de la Raza; while Los Angeles Contemporary Exhibitions [LACE] hosted a performance and video series and an exhibition curated by artists Karen Carson and Jacci Den Hartog.

9
See Lane Relyea, “LA Based and Superstructure,” *Public Offerings* (Los Angeles: Museum of Contemporary Art, Los Angeles, 2001), p. 248–265. Thanks to Jane McFadden for recommending this essay.

10
Ed Leffingwell, *LAX: The Los Angeles Exhibition 1992* (Los Angeles: Directors of the Gallery at Barnsdall Art Park, 1992), p. 23 and 32, emphases in original.

11
Howard Singerman, *Art Subjects: Making Artists in the American University* (Berkeley & Los Angeles: University of California Press, 1999), p. 203 and 260.

12
Martinez cited in Coco Fusco, "My Kind of Conversation: The Public Artworks of Daniel J. Martinez," in *The Things You See When You Don't Have a Grenade* (Santa Monica: Smart Art Press, 1996), p. 21.

13
Gamboa has given artist talks at Harvard, Dartmouth, and Cornell, among other universities. He was also included in the panel for the exhibition *Made in California* at the Los Angeles County Museum of Art (1999). Martinez has presented countless lectures at universities and museums, including at the San Juan Trienal de Poli/graphica (December 2004).

14
Pocho Research Society, "Guerilla Historians Hit LA with (un)Official Historical Markers," press release, May 4, 2002.

15
For more on the history of "urban renewal" projects and their often dire consequences on Mexicano and Mexican-American communities, see Raul H. Villa's *Barrio-Logos, Space and Place in Urban Chicano Literature and Culture* (Austin: University of Texas Press, Austin, 2000).

16
Kenneth Foote, *Shadowed Ground: America's Landscapes of Violence and Tragedy* (Austin: University of Texas Press, 1997), p. 294.

17
For more on the history of Slanguage, see my interview with Juan Capistran and Mario Ybarra, "Eddie Olmos and the Future Conceptualists: An Interview with Juan Capistran and Mario Ybarra Jr.," http://www.latinart.com/faview.cfm

18
Participants at this informal roundtable on July 23, 2004, included: Saul Alvarez, Yanira Cartageña, Ondine Chavoya, Sandra de la Loza, Christina Fernandez, Pete Galindo, Ken Gonzales Day, Rita Gonzalez, Bill Kelley, Daniel J. Martinez, Chon Noriega, Ruben Ortiz Torres, Jorge Nava, Leda Ramos, and Mario Ybarra Jr. Others were invited but could not attend.

19
See Max Benavidez, "Mexican Gothic: A Post-Chicano Aesthetic," unpublished lecture (Foundation for Art Resources, Los Angeles, 1991).

New Locations

inSite: Mapping Borders within Public Culture

Osvaldo Sánchez

InSite is difficult to describe, not because of the vagueness with which it has positioned itself in the international art scene, but because of its rejection of the parameters that order this global environment. "What is inSite?" is a question we are constantly asking ourselves. Since its inception in 1992, inSite has never had a specific structure nor has it focused on pre-conceived practices. inSite has never had its own fixed offices or a long-term staff or a definitive timetable. As an event that appears and disappears, inSite is one of those projects that is easier to explain in terms of what it is not, rather than what it is. inSite is not a biennale. It is not an exhibition. It is not a festival. It is not a collection of site-specific pieces. It is not a residency program. With a budget of three million dollars, it is difficult to call it an alternative contemporary art project. All of these descriptions are inadequate mainly because they do not reveal the real work achieved by the project—in particular, its role as a network that links together unrecognized social flows and constructs new relationships between individuals and institutions, opening up new possibilities of permeability between the two sides of the US-Mexico border. This disposition towards permeability becomes an exercise in culture.

The specificity of inSite comes not from its location on the border but from the relations that each of its works triggers within contexts that are equally specific. Its site-specificity is at the center of an eroded in-between that arrives with the experience of switching, commuting, and circumstantial (un)rooting. inSite seeks to encourage the fluctuation of border limits within all manner of urban experiences, informed by diverse strategies taken from art, anthropology, the heuristic, and the political. Edition after edition, these strategies have arisen not only because of the radical nature of inSite's theoretical framework but often as a result of the dissension that exists among certain artists who are tired of the priorities and expectations associated with the predominant professional practices of the contemporary art scene.

So, for us, envisioning inSite as a network, even if it might seem vague and overly inclusive, is much more in line with this historic project's character as a process, and its actual potential for stimulating interconnections. inSite's main goal has always been divided between a desire to act upon the border context, and a passion for unleashing the mental rebellion that many of us still consider the most surprising qualities of art. On the one hand, these goals can be expressed as the stimulation of models of cultural practices that reveal the political agency of the public domain. And on the other, they offer new alternatives to the current practice of art: a field in which the constrictions and inertia of the market, and the tyranny of the need for novelty in a globalized curatorial arena, are obviated by unusual circumstances of production, placement, and circulation of works.

What are the other aspects of inSite that make it such a unique project? Its initial particularity was the result of a very idiosyncratic initiative generated by two people: Michael Krichman and Carmen Cuenca. For twelve years they have continually ensured that inSite's first priority has always been continual re-invention and faith in the inexhaustible capacity of art to disturb and to surprise. inSite is well-known, not because of its curators or because of international exposure in the art press or because it is has been astute in adopting the latest fashionable artistic trend. inSite's significance is due to the amazing artistic works that it has produced and supported.

It is from this perspective that I want to examine inSite. In what follows I select a few pieces from each edition, consider the circumstances in which they arose and the ways in which they defined each installment of inSite.

1994

Helen Escobedo, *Con la marea nocturna … (By the Night Tide …)*

C*on la marea …* is emblematic of the initial profile of interventions generated by inSite, and in some way, years later, marked the beginning of another model, equally rhetorical, of border art.[1] The artist, Helen Escobedo, is a doyenne of sculpture at the urban scale in open spaces in Mexico. This piece is without doubt one of her most important works. In the extreme northwest of Mexico, on a sandy stretch of Playas Tijuana, Escobedo erected a game, a paranoid fiction, a war machine—strange vessels?—facing the border wall along Friendship Park. These machines seemed almost surprised to find themselves there, to have suddenly appeared by the night tide … They took the form of three steel structures, simulating barges armed with catapults (made of old parabolic antennas) and loaded with coconuts. The barges were called el Topo (the Mole), el Sapo (the Toad), and el Pollo (the Chicken)—parodying the Pinta, the Nina, and the Santa Maria that spearheaded another Conquest, and highlighting the violent fission between identity and territory in the imaginary of this zone. The piece, with its coconuts, fantasizes about a type of economic revenge. For among the street vendors on the Mexican side, it is the coconut stalls that are closest to the border. It was said that a few days later someone had switched the coconuts for rocks … From this perspective, *Con la marea …* was a major leap for inSite.

Three years later, at the time of the 1997 edition, many pieces had abandoned the intention of "installing themselves" or "conversing" from one side of the border, implicitly taking their lead from Escobedo's work. Furthermore, the border is articulated less and less as a territorial marker, and there is less interest in the "critical" potential of a bi-polar nationalist discourse. Is important to note, however, that on its own merit this piece did not fit well with the contemporary concept of site-specificity. Its humor, historical weight, and symbolic call to action, announced a new genealogy for the site-specific agenda of the mid-1990s. Although it was quite photogenic, *Con la marea …* distanced itself from the conventional interventions in a landscape now part of the scenery of Land art.

On the contrary, its metaphors seemed to quote the Situationist strategies that a few years later would distinguish the generalized focus of many interventions in the public arena, where the urban layout is both a weapon to be fired and a bullet-riddled map.

Marcos Ramírez (ERRE), *Century 21*

Commissioned as part of inSITE94, ERRE's *Century 21*, a re-made shack resembling the tattered houses that cover Tijuana's hillsides, brought to light a submerged element of Tijuana history. The Tijuana Cultural Center (CECUT) stands on land that used to be Cartolandia, an illegal shanty town that was swept away in a sea of mud when the Aberlardo Ramírez dam was emptied—whether by accident or, as rumors suggested, prompted by the municipal authorities, no one knows for sure. Once the settlement was buried, it was easier for the state to decommission and appropriate the area, becoming the catalyst for a great wave of real estate speculation. In short order a "master plan" was designed, right in the heart of a central business district and along the major route for border traffic. Taking up these themes, *Century 21* was another important precedent for artistic practice in the area. Its dense critical analysis denied the idea of "specificity" understood as symbolic expansion, or as "cultural branding," at a time when any postmodern gesture—with a mix of low-brow mischief and any textual referent—could easily legitimate an aesthetic artifact on the urban scale. ERRE's piece managed to insert itself as a work of art into a local art scene dominated at this time by modern objects and shackled by the pretensions of manufacturing and authorship. *Century 21*, in its way, reincarnates the political spirit of Chicano activism of the 1970s and 1980s—still vibrant in the historical memory of the region—while avoiding the ethnic paraphernalia and exotic delirium into which it stagnated, even in the political sphere.[2]

Termed "a memorial to a hidden history,"[3] *Century 21* reveals a history of plunder and abuse, long hidden beneath the grandiloquence of many of the state's architectural monuments and institutional symbols of progress. *Century 21* incorporated a sophisticated simulation and a skillful political handling of the deconstructive elements of architecture. The contemporaneity of the piece arises from its avoidance of the ideological framework subtended by the pamphleteering protest and the substitution of a very "specific" reading of the political collusion that exists in the region between memory, territory and community, state and real estate. The building of the CECUT is just one example of constructions that masked the mafia-like network that crosses the government, land speculators, and the businesses that urbanized (and continue to develop) this strategic the zone. *Century 21* created—perhaps for the first time in Mexico—a critical reading of the monuments of centralized power, and unmasked the nexus of political fictions hidden beneath the urban fabric.

1997

Francis Alÿs, *The Loop*

The Loop has a deceptively simple premise: going to Tijuana from San Diego without crossing the border. Alÿs decided to take " ... a route perpendicular to the border wall. I will circumnavigate the earth, leaving from 67 degrees SE, heading NE and then SE again, until returning to my point of departure ... "[4] The project was undertaken between June 1 and 5, 1997.

The Loop was a key piece not just for the artist's career, but for inSite, the region as a whole, as well as for wider art worlds. For inSite, the production of this dérive, without local visibility or verifiable public impact, was something of a challenge. By virtue of its extreme nature, *The Loop* demonstrated the (hitherto rare) ability of inSite to foster pieces without making concessions to any conventional artistic ordering system. In addition, this tour de force resisted the tendency to shackle public art to urban visibility, mass consumption, or spectacle, the most common models with reference to which "the public" is incorporated into an American culture lulled by civic didacticism.

As the imaginary nomad of our global geography, Alÿs enacted a parody of the dimensions of local transit. He circumvented the border territory as his area of action, choosing instead to incarnate the ideas of trajectory, flow, and permeability in an action bereft of any reference to a precise place. In this way, *The Loop* spoke of the possibility of a delocalization of the territorial contents of a "site specific" piece and of how such a delocalization could bear witness to the theatrical essence of the politics of space—through the very absence of place. The Loop made it clear that the political potential of every place is always surpassed by the experiential and ephemeral character of the transits and uses that constantly construct and undo the experience of its specificity.

As a consequence, with inSITE97, the border—long understood according to such indices of superimposed temporalities, trajectories, flows, blockages, and unforeseen permeabilities—was now revealed as an informal laboratory of practices in the public domain, rather than a symbolic enclave of polar and immutable identities.[5]

Andrea Fraser, *Inaugural Speech*

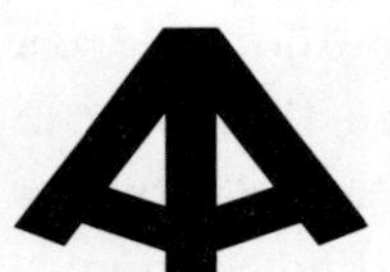nother of the most radical pieces of inSITE97 was also another performance, this one by Andrea Fraser. "Thank you. Thank you. Thank you very much. On behalf of the participating artists—who have actually been seated way in the back ... Hi! ... " As its title indicates, Fraser's work was an enactment of a public speech in the form of a parody of the inaugural ceremony for 1997. An official event of this nature, including public functionaries, was a requirement this year because of the significant participation of the Mexican government. The formalities themselves allowed Andrea to infiltrate the terrain of the political farce and the corporate co-opting of culture, "lauding" the ideal of art as capital in the form of "public well-being." Alluding to the ethical and ideological diatribes that both signal and mask the politics of public participation in art, her *Inaugural Speech* exposed the exhibitionist nature of the unequal levels of commitment that such an act creates. It was an uncomfortable piece, even for inSite, because of the unusual level of confrontation cumulatively provoked from its real and figurative platform—a crucial locus of power for any public event—as it became apparent how she was skewering the protocols of

the inauguration. "As more and more of our Latin American friends are joining our museum boards and country clubs, and purchasing estates in our neighborhoods, we are discovering that we have more in common than art, golf, and horsemanship. There are also political and economic interests that we share. Through cooperative projects such as this we are testing the soil for new hybrids: planting seeds which will blossom into beautiful joint ventures, election victories, and influence on policy throughout the hemisphere."[6]

Inaugural Speech occasioned several warnings and reflections for inSite with respect to its community links, its co-sponsorship alliances, and institutional affiliations; and perhaps without meaning to, ended up demonstrating the strength of its agenda. Clearly, not many events in the contemporary art world could hold up under a test such as this. Fraser's piece unmasked the complex relations—often at their most paradoxical in the discourse of the border—between capital and national identity.

2000–2001

Gustavo Artigas, *Rules of the Game*

This project was conceived around two recreational propositions: a live sporting event and the installation of a frontón—a sort of handball game—court in front of the border wall in Colonia Libertad.

The game: Two indoor soccer teams from Tijuana high schools playing against two high school basketball teams from San Diego. Playing against each other, the two, that is, the four, at the same time, in the same space. A minimum set of rules was established at the beginning to allow the flow of the game. Two dynamics, two balls, two rules, two games, two referees, two narratives, two languages ... in the synchrony of a vital cross-border space.

Artigas' idea was to parody two different dynamics in the context of urban border life. One, the dynamics of coexistence—a friendly game: interacting at the same time in the same place. The second, a dynamic of rejection: situated so close to the border fence, the frontón, with its continuous bounce of the ball against the wall, emblematizes this repetitive opposition—but the project as a whole converts it into experiences of participation and association. Each component demanded different models of group negotiation. In the frontón court, the interactive dynamics were left suspended, subject to spontaneity, as a free social game within the daily life of the Colonia Libertad neighborhood. In the live game, team by team, the dynamic was directed, and allowed one to suppose—as much for the public as the players—that perhaps if that weird game was possible there must also be a way to share the chaos of these different border experiences superimposed in time and space.

"Making the wall bigger, allowing the people to play," as Artigas put it, the piece sought to find a positive interaction with the wall in everyday life. Artigas proposed the recuperation of this mistake which is the wall, taking advantage of its bouncing energy, making the no-access a resource for the political construction of a sense of belonging to the community—using play that weaves unexpected relations into the heart of a tough neighborhood.[7]

For the public, following the performance of the game guaranteed an understanding of the political force of the heuristic impulse in this "impossible" activity, whose unpredictability and certainty underline the very mechanisms that determine and secure the border. Even though it was based on the parody of nameless rules, the group awareness in this live participation led to an understanding of the border as a flux with its logic molded by the possible—which leads to an important implication of the piece in its political commitment to open exchange.[8]

Generating a liberating experience between a heterogeneous audience in unusual circumstances, *Rules of the Game* unreservedly exposed the political capacity of the heuristic as the logic of live self-construction of the public and its domain. Somehow this project employed models of participation and problem solving that have the structure of a social game and used the identification mechanisms associated with spectator sports. Heuristics, here, underlies artistic experience as a process that generates knowledge from a sensory experience constructed as social fiction. Its liberating capacity lies in the potential to assist in the self-reproduction of the collective subject through an experience that reveals "the possible." As one of the curators for inSITE2000, I was particularly struck by works that engaged these kind of strategies. It was this

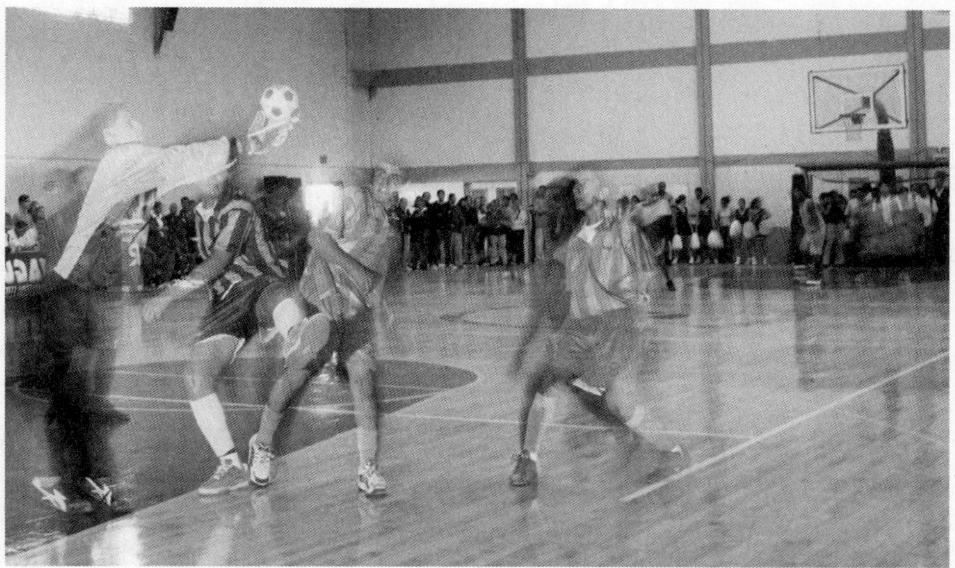

COURTESY OF INSITE

Gustavo Artigas
The Rules of the Game, 2000–2001
Still from the Video-document of the performance
inSITE2000–2001

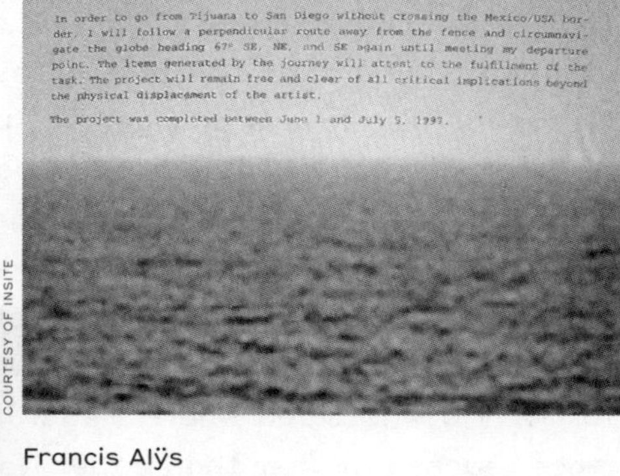

COURTESY OF INSITE

Francis Alÿs
The Loop, 1997
Printed card, document of performance-action
inSITE97

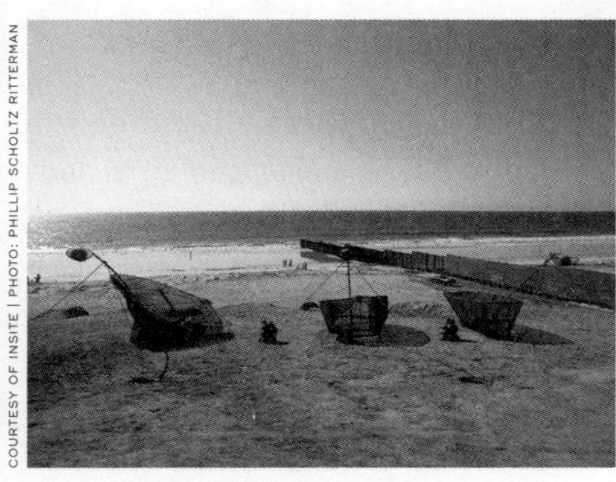

COURTESY OF INSITE | PHOTO: PHILLIP SCHOLTZ RITTERMAN

Helen Escobedo
Con la marea nocturna ... , 1994
Playas de Tijuana, Tijuana
Installation View
inSITE94

experience as a simple spectator, even more than my experience as a co-curator of the project, that made me think about the limits between art, language, and experience. It is precisely these limits that the curatorial statement of 2005 aims to challenge within the framework of contemporary popular culture.

Mark Dion, *Blind/Hide*

At first sight, the work of Mark Dion might be seen as a poetic construction, of limited "use," set-up in a remote area that is difficult to reach. A bird-watching blind in the middle of the Tijuana River estuary rather than "public art," or even than "art," it appeared on one view merely as the extravagance of a bird lover, offering only a hardly-detectable metaphoric relation to the nearby training ground for helicopter pilots. Facing the fresh water that flows toward the coast where birds nest, the blind was equipped with all the information and accoutrements necessary to generate a memorable experience for bird lovers and general public. Of course the piece can also be interpreted from an art-world point of view as launching a series of critical parodies, between the ecological reserve and the military pilots, between bird watching and military surveillance, between the belligerent and obsessive maneuvers of the helicopters and the barely perceptible routines of the migratory birds in what is now an ecological reserve and formerly a wasteland where illegal immigrants were persecuted. Yet the piece reaches further than either its embrace of a welcome and sufficient territory, or its rediffusion across a symbolic zone. To understand Dion's piece as a site-specific installation with a didactic function, it is enough to regard the loving detail of its interior and the romantic vision it presents. *Blind/Hide* however is aligned more with public art than community service; it is more than a facility for pensioners who love watching birds, or children taking introductory courses on animal habitat and ecological systems. For the work reclaims the ground of intimacy, informed by serene and curious motivation, focused on a visibility that uses the everyday as a veil, and the experience of contact with an evident promise of recreation. *Blind/Hide*, then, is made present only to be unveiled—viewed, interviewed—as an "artwork," without relying on any of the indicators of presence or the procedures of participation and reward that characterize what is still considered "public art" in today's culture.

The works of Artigas and Dion also share certain characteristics with other pieces produced for inSITE2000—a congruence that, for me, revealed an emerging detour in the practice, not only of public art, but of art in general. On the one hand, I like to think that these works understand public art as an experience, in real times and spaces, where the subject—the artist included—discovers himself or herself to be a modest activator of a social contract that is always in flux. This results in an unaccustomed experience in which the efforts of the artist subvert the context of the artwork—all that constitutes the living domain and political belonging of the public. On the other hand, I think that both pieces react to a latent discontent with the extreme degree of overexposure and mass consumption of works of art, with their emblematization as corporate indicators, and all that follows from this—the vulgarization of the models of interchange between work and individual, the abusive substitutions between public space and public domain, and the heartless exploitation of artists as a supplier of new brands for a bulimic market. In Artigas, the performance-oriented nature of the piece hardly rewards us with the competitive and mythical compulsion of the spectacle—premised on the cultural hero—craved by certain audiences. While in Dion, the intimate experience of this "minor" intervention is predicated on concerns quite distant from the routines of daily consumption. It utterly refuses the exaltation of a product the public must buy—or consume—as an accessory that guarantees their social status as good citizens (typical of most contemporary artistic production), substituting a surprise appearance that stimulates the wild energy of something that still has not been converted into a brand.

inSite_05

The aim of inSite_05 is to create experiences of the public domain. By that I mean generating collective situations that transform the circumstantial negotiation of the uses of space and zones of instability into a process that reveals the vision of the social structure in its totality as a new political network. inSite_05 envisions the city as a social fabric whose survival is dependent on its flows. As a result, it strives to stimulate novel experiences of the public domain and to implement alternative modes of interconnectedness. Many of its "public art" works will be almost impossible to track down or locate as visible "monuments" within the urban grid. The real aim of inSite_05 resides primarily in recovering the power of specific heuristic strategies, in particular, game-playing and fictional narratives, which have a long history of interaction with art practice and can be held, in some circumstances, to constitute that which is understood as artistic. Such strategies include the invention of subversive fables, ephemeral representations, buzzy marketing, environmental experimentation, the public dissemination of informational archives, parodies of political events and mass spectacle, the generation of models of affiliation and community consensus, or records of everyday acts of cultural resistance, and so on. By means of the critical processes entailed in these strategies, and the delineation of dénouements that involve participating individuals, inSite_05 will make tangible the experience of the "public" as a coming together of social subjects.

Notes

1
The type of installation prevalent at the beginning of the 1990s, so effective symbolically for their location in the heart of a territory of collisions and political protests—and usually rather easy to instigate—assisted in the spread of a rhetoric of "site-specific" through the border area that almost always accommodates the (re)presentation of emblems of identity.

2
It is difficult historically to contextualize the works fostered by inSite without mentioning precursors in the SD/TJ area that linked artistic practice to the border flows, debates about identity, and strategies of citizen appropriation of the urban fabric. For a well-documented account of artistic practice in the region during the last four decades, see Jo-Anne Berelowitz, "Border Art since 1965," *Postborder City*, eds. Michael Dear and Gustavo Leclerc (New York: Routledge, 2003).

3
Olivier Debroise, "By the Night Tide/ inSITE94," *inSITE94*, exh. cat., Installation Gallery, San Diego, 1995.

4
Francis Alÿs, "The Loop," *Private Time in Public Space. inSITE97*, exh. cat., Installation Gallery, San Diego, 1998.

5
Of course any effective political exercise in the space of this border region implies at a minimum the establishment of hierarchies from the point of view of site, each of which negotiates its distance from any national construction of history and identity. "Naming" the site—not according to its identifying indices, its territory as a symbolic possession but with reference to an experiential negotiation of all the identifying intermittencies (all those masks of circumstantial visibility and invisibility)—allows the cracks in the power structure to be manifested.

6
Andrea Fraser, "Inaugural Speech," *Private Time in Public Space. inSITE97*, exh. cat., Installation Gallery, San Diego, 1998.

7
The deterioration of the court and the transformation of its uses since 2000 have been surprising. It has served as a mixed-function frontón and basketball court, as a platform for art, showing junked cars that have been artistically reinterpreted; while just few months ago, neighbors began to place plants around it and along the wall, turning this edge of hell into a rarified garden.

8
Artigas intuitively used the heuristic as a model for the construction of the "public" in everyday urban experience. Heuristics underlies artistic experience as a process that generates knowledge from a sensory experience constructed as social fiction. In heuristics, "the possible"—exhibited as an underlying dynamic of subsystems in conflict—refers to the (in)stability of any (social) structure and frames the production of new (social) subjects who are made aware their own interaction.

A Guided Tour of the Center for Land Use Interpretation

Matthew Coolidge and Erik Knutzen

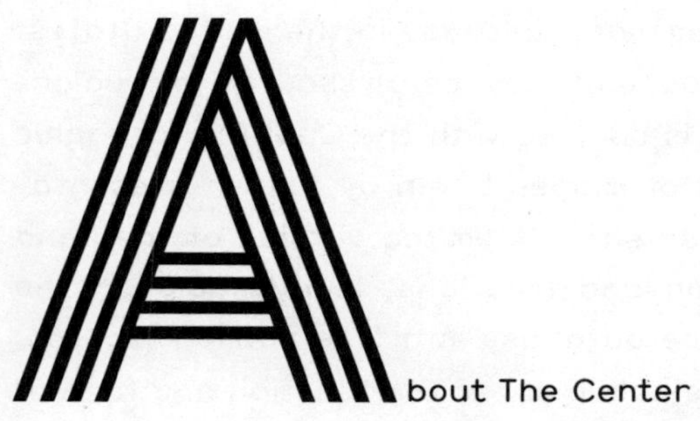

About The Center

The Center for Land Use Interpretation (CLUI) is a research organization interested in understanding the nature and extent of human interaction with the earth's surface. The Center's stated mission is to "increase and diffuse information about how the nation's lands are apportioned, utilized, and perceived." The Center embraces a multidisciplinary approach to fulfilling this mission, employing conventional research and information-processing methodologies as well as nontraditional interpretive tools. The organization was founded in 1994, and since that time has produced many exhibits on land-use themes and regions for public institutions throughout the United States, as well as internationally. Public tours have been conducted in several states, and CLUI has published more than ten books.

The Center exists to stimulate discussion, thought, and general interest in the contemporary landscape. Neither an environmental group nor an industry-affiliated organization, the work of the Center integrates many approaches to land-use—the multiple perspectives of the landscape—into a single vision that illustrates the common ground in land-use debates. At the very least, the Center attempts to emphasize the multiplicity of points of view regarding the utilization of terrestrial and geographic resources.

Land Use Database

At the core of the Center's methodology is the Land Use Database, a collection of source material and processed information on unusual and exemplary land-use in the United States. The database is used in-house at CLUI as a resource for regional and thematic programming, and is coupled with the CLUI Photographic Archive, a collection of thousands of images taken by CLUI representatives, covering all types of land-use sites. A limited version of the Land Use Database, with over one thousand locations, is available on the internet at www.clui.org. The on-line database is a free public resource, designed to educate and inform the public about the function and form of the national landscape.

Some sites included in the database are works by government agencies involved in geo-transformative activities, such as the Department of Energy, the Bureau of Reclamation, the Army Corps of Engineers, and the Department of Defense. Also included are industrially altered landscapes, such as especially noteworthy mining sites, features of transportation systems, and field test facilities for a variety of high-impact technologies. The database includes museums and displays related to land-use, and one of the most thorough listings of land art sites available. The database describes these sites, and offers links for more detailed information. In many cases information on how to visit these sites is provided, so that they may be directly experienced. The database is continuously being updated by increasing the number of sites listed and expanding the information it contains.

Programs and Projects

The Center produces public exhibits on themes and regions for galleries and museums, as well as for exhibition in CLUI venues in Los Angeles and elsewhere, and conducts public bus tours and educational field trips. Usually these tours are led by the CLUI on video-equipped buses, as part of a CLUI Exhibition Program. Lectures and presentations are held at CLUI's exhibition spaces, through programs such as the Independent Interpreter series, which is an ongoing series of presentations by selected artists and researchers whose work might be of special interest to CLUI's audience. These presentations take the form of evening lectures with slides or films, or an exhibition of material, and sometimes both. Other programming includes site-specific Extrapolative Projects in the field, and special focus thematic study areas. The Center also publishes guidebooks, catalogs, and other books addressing land-use issues. These publications, and selected titles from other publishers, are available through the CLUI store in Los Angeles and at the organization's online shop. The Center also publishes a newsletter, *The Lay of the Land*, which is distributed to interested parties worldwide.

The Center engages in a number of interpretive projects in the field that are designed to draw meaning from land-use sites and phenomena. Many of these projects represent extensions of traditional interpretive techniques, and are designed to expand the methodology into new fronts. Extrapolative Projects can be ongoing or momentary, physically realized, or in the design stage. They include outdoor displays and signage, site-specific interactions, and other permanent or ephemeral activities. Some projects can be considered as a sort of "R&D" of interpretive practice at the Center.

An example of one of CLUI's Extrapolative Projects is the Event Marker Project in which a series of markers, similar to roadside markers installed by historical organizations, that commemorate significant but obscure land-use phenomena, have been installed at numerous locations around the United States. Several themes are being explored, including Inundations and Denudations, Perpetual Flames, and Selected Film Location Sites. As part of the Peculiar Detonations series, for example, markers have been placed at an accidental H-Bomb Impact Site in New Mexico, and at the site on the Oregon Coast where a car was crushed by flying whale blubber as part of a beached whale disposal attempt.

The Center's main exhibition space and offices in Los Angeles houses exhibits, lectures, and other resources for the public. The Center's library and archives are available to researchers by appointment and docents are available to address classes and groups. Project support facilities exist at the Center's Wendover, Utah, complex which houses a residency program, and at the Desert Research Station (DRS) near Barstow, California. The DRS is a research and display facility located in the Mojave desert, acting as a satellite to the Los Angeles location, and focusing on the California Desert region.

The Center's Bus Tours provide a way to give our audience a direct experience of the landscape. An example of one of the many bus tours the Center has conducted is a visit to the industrial city of Irwindale, east of Los Angeles, which was conducted as part of the exhibition *Ground Up: Photographs of the Ground in the Margins of Los Angeles*. The tour, entitled "Margins in Our Midst, A Journey Into Irwindale," was about the material that makes up the ground on which we live and featured visits to the gravel and aggregate mining pits that continue to provide the concrete and asphalt that is spread on Los Angeles' roads, as well as the raw material for the city's major construction projects.

Thematic Program Areas

Thematic Program Areas are subject categories that have been selected for extended research and examination by CLUI. Selected themes are studied as ongoing projects, with findings periodically presented to the public in the form of publications, lectures, exhibits, or other programs.

Model Earth

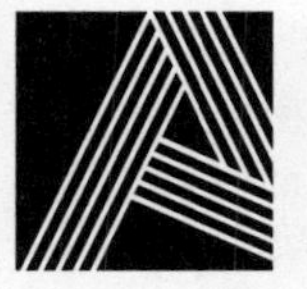n example of one of the Center's Thematic Programs is our interest in models, maps, globes, and other stylized representations of the earth or portions of the earth's surface that are part of the phenomenon of terrestrial miniaturization. Such representations often say much about how we see, or want to see, the world. Some fascinating examples of these phenomena include the utilitarian models created for hydrologic studies by the United States Army Corps of Engineers, the world's premier functional terrestrial model makers. The three largest hydrologic models in the world are located in the United States, and the Center has developed exhibits about each. *Model of Decay: The Chesapeake Bay Model*, was an exhibition of images and artifacts from this massive miniature working model of the Chesapeake Bay. Now abandoned and decaying, this was once the largest indoor hydraulics model in the world. The second exhibit on this theme was *Mississippi Model*, which assembled images and artifacts from this 200 acre outdoor installation—currently the largest hydraulics model in the world, but now abandoned and overgrown outside of Jackson, Mississippi. Our *Model Limits: The San Francisco Bay Model* exhibit was a photo documentary of the "San Francisco Bay-Delta Tidal Hydraulic Model," a two-acre working model of the San Francisco Bay Area.

Guide Points

Direct experience of places beyond the familiar limits of one's local community is often obtained as a tourist. Whether one is self-guided through the landscape by tour books, or on a programmatic excursion under the direction of a tour guide, this kind of experience both enriches and confuses the traveler's sense of the places they visit. Points of interest along a tourist route have an apparent heightened relevance, while the tourist often feels a sense of somewhat disturbing passivity, having relinquished control to someone else. This state of being, and the industry that promotes it, is of interest to all of us who have "been there."

CLUI developed the guide point theme in an exhibit about postcard entrepreneur Merle Porter, a one-man postcard production company producing and distributing millions of cards over a 50-year career. Nearly always about places, his cards have a distinctive style, sometimes depicting famous sites, but more often a sort of celebration of the ordinary landscape: highways, abandoned buildings, and oil fields. Typically his route took him through the California, Arizona, and Nevada desert areas in winter, and the California beach areas in summer. At the height of his career, Porter was putting 1,000 miles a week on his Ford Econoline van (which served both as living quarters and portable inventory room), and circulating one million cards a year, under the name Royal Pictures of Colton, California.

Above Ground

The relationship between land-use and the sky is the subject of this thematic program area. From aerial observations of the ground, to mountaintop observatories that gaze out into space, land and sky are linked in many ways The electronosphere, the infrastructure of the information age, is an invisible realm, often tangible only at the physical sites, such as antennas and earthstations, where waves make contact with the earth.

This theme was explored in the Center's VORs of Texas exhibit. VOR (Very high frequency Omnidirectional Radial) antennas are radio beacons, part of a nationwide network of navigational aids used by civil and military aviation. While their function is consistent, their shapes and coloration can vary, and their enigmatic forms hint at the all-too-unfamiliar parallel universe of communication technologies. The exhibit was a typological photographic research project exploring the context and form of all the some 70 VOR antennas in the state of Texas, and included a color photograph of each. It was the product of the field research and photography of CLUI researcher and Texas Projects Coordinator Mark Curtin.

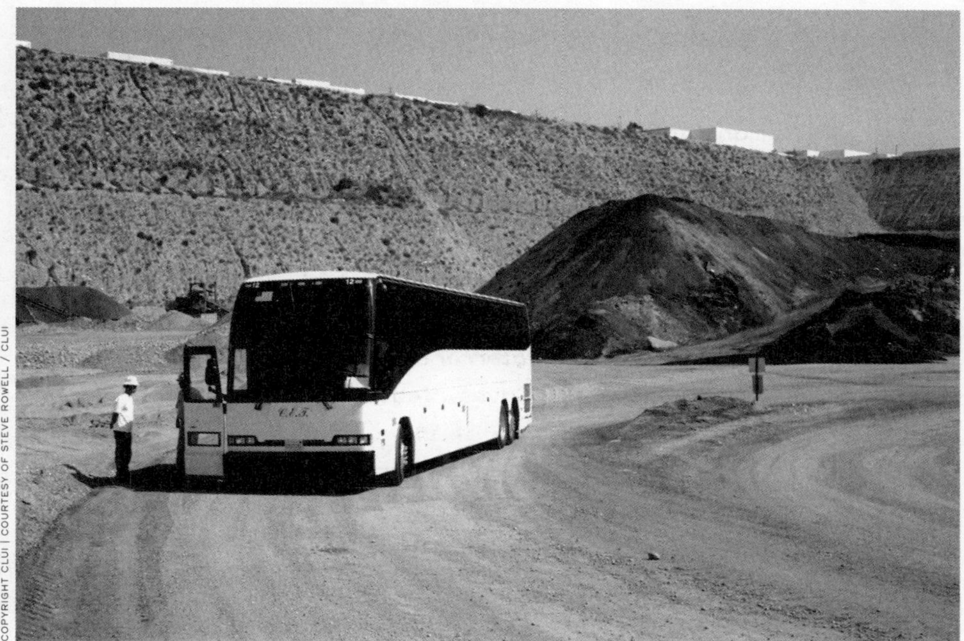

Center For Land Use Interpretation (CLUI) Tour bus in a gravel pit in Irwindale, California, during the "Margins in Our Midst" tour, 2003

Under Ground

Human interaction with the land often extends beyond the earth's superficia veneer, into the underground. Whether things are located underground for spatial or climatic reasons, for secrecy or security, or simply by chance, an examination of this realm can give a sense of what lurks in the fundament of the country, and provide an indirect "overview" of what exists on the surface.

The Center's exhibit, *Subterranean Renovations: The Unique Architectural Spaces of Show Caves*, featured color photographs of 12 of the most compelling examples of this unique form of underground architecture. Represented were the lunchrooms at Carlsbad Caverns and Mammoth Cave, light show theaters at DeSoto and Meramec Caverns, the reception room at Truitt Cave, with its working fireplace, the abandoned bandstand and dance floor, deep within Wonderland Cave and Club in Bella Vista, Arkansas, and the haunting Stalacpipe Organ at Luray Caverns, Virginia.

Mediated Space

In this media age, much of our experience of places and landscapes is filtered through the productions of the entertainment and advertising industries, such as films, television, and commercial photography. This thematic program area examines representations of place through the lens of these mediated perspectives.

Two recent CLUI exhibitions, *On Locations: Places as Sets in the Landscape of Los Angeles* and *Emergency State: First Responder and Law Enforcement Training Architecture* examined mediated space, or what Los Angeles cultural critic, Norman Klein calls "Scripted Space." *On Locations* featured images, text, and a multimedia display about the film location industry, focusing on how places within the public realm can be transformed, physically and contextually, by the moving-image industries of film, television, and advertising. Within the spectrum of façades, streetscapes, and structures that are used as locations, are certain spaces that vividly embody (both physically and theoretically) this paradox of place, and reveal (subtly or otherwise) the intriguing dynamic between “real” and “cinematic” space.

Emergency State, about police and emergency training structures, featured images taken by CLUI photographers depicting ten representative locations in Southern California. The region’s training villages and emergency props range from modest buildings to entire towns, complete with simulated convenience stores, apartments, and gas stations supplied by a level of realism in tune with a location long associated with the movie industry and the origins of theme parks. The training sites depicted exhibit different characteristics of this unusual form of architecture, which is increasing in both numbers and sophistication across the country—as the era of “preparedness” progresses.

As with several recent exhibits at the Center, this one was a digitally created and displayed production, with each of the sites described on a LCD or projection screen, along with printed text panels, enhanced by video and ambient sound.

Site Lines

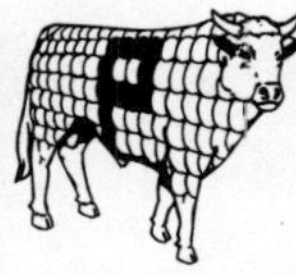

erimeters and cartographic grids constitute a network of overlying lines on the landscape delimiting the margins or intersections of places. The Site Lines thematic program area examines the edges of places, which are often distinct locations in themselves, and the interaction of physical place with conceptual lines. The structures that emerge along linear transpositions, such as fences, berms, and signage, are part of this land-use language.

CLUI’s photo-documentary project, *The Limits of Fun*, examined site lines by documenting the perimeters of theme parks, examining the physical and social structures at the fringes of these recreational land use zones.

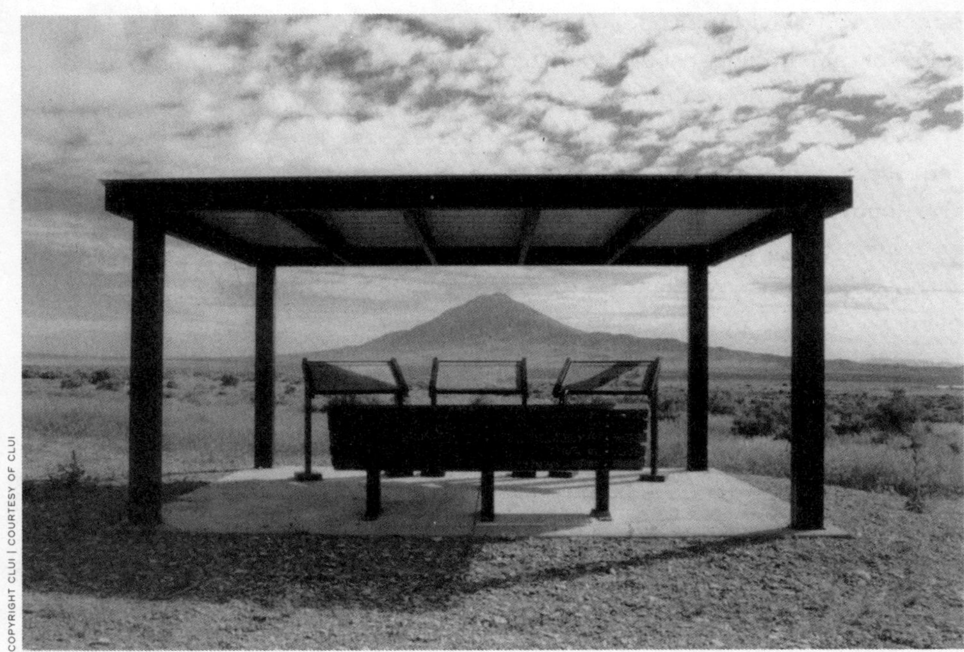

Center For Land Use Interpretation (CLUI)
Pilot Peak interpretative rest stop, 1997

Erosive Forces

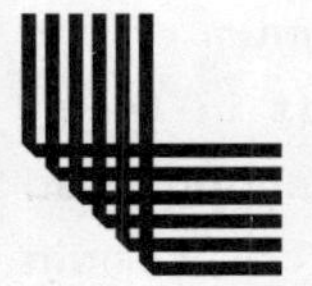

andscape change is due largely to erosion, the gradual breaking down of landforms into small particles which seek the lowest energy state. Counteracting erosional decay are certain building forces that pile things up, such as tectonics, as well as the human agents of landscape change, including architecture, drainage control, landscaping, and paving. The interaction of human changes with the landscape and erosion is the subject of this special CLUI program theme.

Two CLUI exhibitions, *Formations of Erasure: Earthworks and Entropy* and *Ground-Up: Photographs of the Ground in the Margins of Los Angeles*, focused on the theme of erosive forces. *Formations of Erasure* consisted of contemporary photographs of earthworks from across the United States, focusing on those that do not have extensive maintenance programs, such as Robert Smithson's *Spiral Jetty* (1971, Great Salt Lake, Utah) and Michael Heizer's *Double Negative* (1969, Mormon Mesa, Overton, Nevada) and thus have been altered by time and the elements. Most of the depicted pieces were constructed in the 1970s and, over time, the intentions, conception, and first articulation of the artist have been modified into dynamic new forms that represent a collaboration between the human and the nonhuman worlds.

Ground-Up used soil maps of Los Angeles County as a tool for reexamining regional physio-geographic phenomena. These curiously compelling maps provide a unique view of the landscape, and of the human interventions across it. The exhibit featured several large-format photographs of selected ground locations. The fine grain of the photographs matched the grain of the depicted ground, and the authority and weight that large, finely crafted images convey contrasted implicitly with the non-places that filled the frame of each exposure, suggesting to some a possible terminus of one limb of the tree of landscape photography.

Isolate Zones

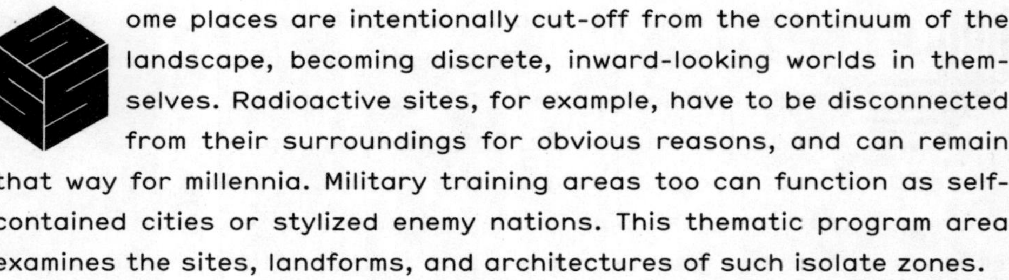

Some places are intentionally cut-off from the continuum of the landscape, becoming discrete, inward-looking worlds in themselves. Radioactive sites, for example, have to be disconnected from their surroundings for obvious reasons, and can remain that way for millennia. Military training areas too can function as self-contained cities or stylized enemy nations. This thematic program area examines the sites, landforms, and architectures of such isolate zones.

The CLUI exhibit *The Nellis Range Complex: Landscape of Conjecture* explored the Isolate Zone theme and was installed inside a customized mobile exhibition unit. The culmination of more than three years of research and photography, the exhibit contained images, text, maps, and supporting documents that describe this mysterious landscape in Southern Nevada, the nation's largest restricted area, and a veritable nation unto itself. Two thousand miles of roads and an extensive fiber-optic and microwave communication network connect target areas, maintenance facilities, tracking stations, testing grounds, and a few full-scale bases and R&D centers. An evolving interactive, simulated enemy landscape, with command and control bunkers, radar and missile sites, convoys, railways, industrial areas, and hundreds more individual targets, trains pilots for confrontations in Middle Eastern, Asian, Soviet, and other potential theaters of war. On the undisturbed mountains within the Range there is a landscape frozen in 1940, when it was first closed to public access, on which bighorn sheep and wild horses roam among petroglyphs of the Paiute and Shoshone Indians, and where miners' cabins remain unvandalized, with glass jars still sitting on their shelves.

Residence Program

In addition to developing internally-produced programs, the Center assists other individuals and organizations in research with a residence program to support the development of new interpretive methodologies and ideas. The program is open to artists, researchers, theorists, or anyone who works with land and land-use issues in an innovative and engaging manner. During the course of the residency, participants are asked to produce work that explores themes related to the area, which will then be exhibited. Residents primarily work out of the CLUI facilities at Wendover, Utah, and explore and interpret the landscape of that remarkable desert region.

Wendover is a small town on the edge of the mountains and salt flats and sits directly on the Utah/Nevada border, on Interstate 80 at the point where the Basin and Range of Nevada spill into the Great Salt Lake Desert of Utah. In appearance it resembles the Arctic: a remote place of barren rock and snow-white alkali. Wendover was established because it was out of the way, a place where people wouldn't want to live. Though there was a small community to service the railroad established early on at Wendover, the first major modern settlement was an airbase, built at the beginning of World War II to train bomber crews (including the crew of the Enola Gay). Through the 1940s and 50s, the land around Wendover was bombed, strafed, and dusted with chemical and biological agents.

Today, though the region is remote, it is intensely industrialized. Military operations continue in the three million surrounding acres of restricted-access lands. Large-scale industries remove salt, and process minerals from the flats, and copper and gold are extracted from giant pits in the mountains. Hazardous waste facilities and obsolete chemical weapons have found refuge in the remote, nearly uninhabitable landscape.

The interstate makes Wendover a pit stop for travelers from San Francisco to New York City, and points in between. The town is bisected by the state line, creating two distinct halves: The gambling boom town of Nevada's West Wendover adjoins the stagnated Utah half, which is dominated by the cluttered remains of the airbase, abandoned by the military in 1977.

It is at this former airbase that the Center for Land Use Interpretation has established the Wendover Residence Program and a segment of the American Land Museum. The sites used by the Center in Wendover and its environs comprise the CLUI Wendover Complex.

In addition to exhibition, R&D, storage, and other facilities, the Center leases a portion of the former military airfield known as South Base, one mile into the flats from the airport flight line. These structures remain from the munitions storage and atomic bomb program at Wendover, with some recent additions, including the control tower, built by the Walt Disney Company (for a film called Con Air, dir. Simon West, 1997). Military and law enforcement personnel conduct "SWAT" team-type training in some of the buildings, including those leased by the CLUI.

The so-called "Remote Location" is a 40-acre piece of land 40 miles north of Wendover, available for projects addressing issues of isolation, accessible most of the year by high-clearance vehicle only. The parcel has a varied topography, extending from a dry lake-bed surface, up a slope to a level plateau, offering views of the Silver Island Mountains to the east and south. It was the first Utah property purchased by Robert Smithson and Nancy Holt.

The American Land Museum

The Center for Land-Use Interpretation is the lead agency in the establishment of the American Land Museum. The purpose of the museum is to create a dynamic contemporary portrait of the nation, composed of the national landscape itself. To establish this far-flung museum, the country has been divided into separate zones called Interpretive Units. Each unit is to have a museum location to represent it, providing regional programming for the area it represents. Interpretive Units were created out of the continuous national fabric through an accumulation of criteria, and finally actualized through the process of combining "districts" and "regions."

Regions are general topographic and land use areas with gradual or transitional boundaries. They generally follow physio-geographic features (such as mountain ranges, and drainage systems), as well as cultural, economic, and historical development patterns (which are often delimited by physiography). Regions could be described as being defined from within, rather than from without, as their edges are often indistinct, overlapping and dissolving into one another. Unambiguous boundaries were then drawn around these regions, following the existing political boundaries that separate states. The cluster of states define the District that makes up each Interpretive Unit.

The physical form of the individual museum locations will differ according to site considerations and available development resources. The primary "exhibit" at each location is, naturally, the immediate landscape of the location. As other interpretive exhibits are prepared for the location, they will be installed in structures that reflect the architectural styles of the region, and usually occupy existing structures. Collectively, the individual exhibition sites comprise the American Land Museum, a museum both situated in and made up of the landscapes of America.

Zero Art in Tijuana?

Marcos Ramírez ERRE and Teddy Cruz

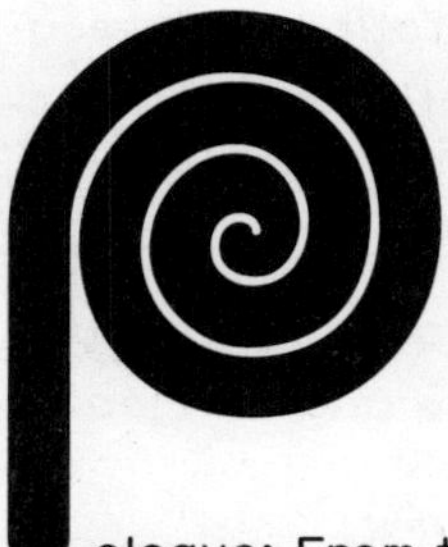

Prologue: From the New Global Border ... To the San Diego-Tijuana Checkpoint, and Back

If we traced an imaginary line extending the US-Mexico border directly across a world atlas as a sort of new political equator, it would directly coincide with the post-9/11 geography of the world revised according to the Pentagon's new map. With its renovated border geographies, the Pentagon re-conceptualizes the perennial division of the world between northern and southern hemispheres—between first and third worlds, generally speaking—into what the Pentagon now calls a distinction between a "Functioning Core" and the "Non-Integrated Gap." It is across this global border that the most dramatic socio-economic global dynamics are taking place as a series of hemispheric double-crossings. On the one hand, an increasing migration of people across this border flows illegally from the "Non-Integrated Gap" searching for the "strong" economies of the "Functioning Core," in a sort of colonization in reverse. While on the other, the redistribution of centers of manufacturing and production moves in the opposite direction, as the "Functioning Core" targets various sites within the "Non-Integrated Gap" to enact its politics of "out-sourcing," searching for the world's cheapest labor markets. Dotted along this line in the form of a sort of "necklace of conflict" are some of the most contested critical thresholds in our current global socio-political geography—among them the Tijuana-San Diego border, the most intensely populated immigration funnel from Latin America into the US; the Straits of Gibraltar, a maritime border where many of the waves of North African migration flow into Europe; and the border between Israel and Palestine, which physically and emblematically demarcates the most dramatic border space in the Middle East.

It is at critical junctures such as the San Diego/Tijuana border region where the shifting cultural demographics and mutating socio-economic forces around the world can be reflected and anticipated, transforming our notions of community, city, and territory. By zooming into the particularities of this volatile territory, we can travel back and forth between these two border cities, exposing their landscapes of contradiction where conditions of difference and sameness collide and overlap on a daily basis.

The international border between the US and Mexico at the San Diego/Tijuana checkpoint is the most trafficked in the world. Approximately 60 million people cross it annually, moving untold amounts of goods and services back and forth. This contested zone is the site of massive contradictions, defined and re-defined every day by the unstable balance between two powerful forces. On one side are the "legal" actions and "official" urban policy prompting the post-9/11 US federal government to rethink surveillance infrastructure, while on the other, insurgent and "illegal" actions proliferate in both border cities in small-scale, spontaneous occupations and appropriations that seek to blur and transgress the ten-foot-high steel wall that divides the border conurbations.

Brief back and forth tours into Tijuana and San Diego can reveal the nature of these contradictions, the double paradox of a trans-border urban cluster that wants to be divided and fluid simultaneously. As we move through these border cities, we witness two different attitudes towards the urban environment. If San Diego is emblematic of an urbanism of segregation and control epitomized by the master-planned and gated communities that define its sprawl, Tijuana's periphery has evolved as a collection of informal, nomadic settlements or favelas. This comparison is not reductive, especially if we consider that the steel border wall is the ultimate symbol of a puritan planning tradition made of social exclusion and separation.

The contrast between these two cities is further dramatized by the unfolding of their different histories, narratives, and identities. Only 20 minutes apart, their centers, for example, represent entirely different socio-economic and political universes. While San Diego calls itself "America's Finest City," Tijuana is viewed in Mexico as a decadent hybrid and transient world unto itself, distinct from (and somehow inferior to) the rest of the country. While San Diego has always been perceived in the US as a picturesque resort town, a point of arrival for migrating populations looking for a nice *cul-de-sac* in which to retire, Tijuana has traditionally been perceived in Mexico as a threshold leading to the "other side," a contemporary Sodom and Gomorrah.

If we consider such contrasts to be the essential characteristics of these divided cities, we can also witness their incremental juxtaposition. The manifold differences between San Diego and Tijuana begin to dwindle as San Diego's signature mini-malls and MacMansions spring up on Tijuana's periphery, and the random patterns of density, mixed-use, and informal economies typical of Tijuana begin to appear in San Diego's inner city. The following mini-tours will reveal how, as these cities further divide, they also begin to contain each other. Unavoidably, in every "first world" city a "third world" exists, and every "third world" city replicates the first.

Border Tours:
Beige Houses, Moving Houses, Houses of Desire (six mini-tours)

Tour 1 *North and South at Zero Set Back: A Chronology of the Wall*

As at other stages in its history, the intensity of the socio-cultural and economic funnel that converges at this border is once more being suppressed as the US federal government is quietly planning to close the gaps and fortify or "harden" the San Diego/Tijuana border checkpoint. This is how one of the most recent and symbolic post-9/11 urban intervention is focusing on the massive transformation of the San Ysidro border crossing, currently in its early planning stages. It is with this project that the department of Homeland Security is pouring billions of dollars into the border region in order to reinforce its infrastructure of surveillance, continuing further to divide the US from its Mexican neighbor.

The massive transformation of the border ecology inspires a chronological retracing of the border's evolution, as well as of the urbanisms that have emerged from this zero set back condition; a recording of how in the last thirty years the invisible line, rendered arbitrarily at one point in history, has incrementally been solidified. The physical transformations of this edge range from a time when the landscape between Tijuana and San Ysidro was uninterrupted (we recall the photographs of Alex Webb showing the area of the border at Colonia Libertad (Freedom Neighborhood) in the early 1970s without a fence, and children flying kites across it, oblivious of any political boundary) to the construction of the first chain link fence, to the erection of a ten-foot-high steel wall built in the early 1990s with leftover temporary landing mats used in operation "Desert Storm" in Kuwait. Since the steel wall has proven to be very inefficient (its corrugation runs horizontally, allowing people to climb it quite easily, and its solidity makes it a perfect place to hide), it is currently being replaced by a more functional version. The newest wall, under construction in 2005, could be called the longest panopticon in history: a very hygienic and efficient wall, made of strategically spaced concrete columns allowing for maximum surveillance and minimum human slippage, crowned by an electrified fence.

Needless to say, the impact of this hardening of the border zone falls first and foremost on the adjacent communities of San Ysidro and Tijuana, not to mention the natural ecology and landscape of their shared territory. These new protectionist strategies, fueled by a collective obsession with safety and security, paranoia and greed, are defining a radically conservative cultural agenda that is incrementally reinforcing a rigid grid of containment, instead of a fluid bed of opportunity. In other words, the fortifying of the wall has occurred in tandem with the underscoring of social legislation toward the public, producing an urban policy of discrimination, exclusion and division. This is how the perennial alliance between militarization and urbanization is reenacted here and epitomized by the solidifying of the border wall that divides these cities, further transforming San Diego into the world's largest gated community.

But despite the apocalyptic implications of a more fortified border and an intensified surveillance infrastructure, the growing tension between the various communities of San Diego and those of Tijuana have elicited a multitude of insurgent responses—new opportunities for constructing alternative modes of encounter for dialogue and debate, sharing resources and infrastructure, recycling at the most outlandish levels the fragments and situations of these two cities and constructing critical practices of encroachment into the increasing privatization of the public realm.

Tour 2 *North = South? Monuments and Anti-Monuments*

Horse

On the 26th of September 1997, as part of a bi-national art project called InSite, Tijuana artist Marcos Ramírez ERRE, rolled an enormous Janus-headed Trojan horse into the midst of traffic waiting to cross the border on both sides. The horse appeared out of nowhere, and in the same way, it vanished. It was positioned to straddle the border, with two legs resting on the US side, one head looking north, while the other legs remained rooted in Mexico, the other head gazing southward. ERRE inserted his horse into the de-centered, de-territorialized, and multi-directional flows that constitute the border, where it dwelled for a brief moment, (impossibly) occupying both sides at once in defiance of the dialectical forces that govern the space. Representing both arrival and departure, stasis as well as movement at a crossroads, Tijuana's horse occupied the ambiguity of the void and in so doing detonated the full potential of the border city from which it emerged, emblematically deploying strategies of appropriation and transgression.

The Doll

In 1989, Armando Muñoz, a favela dweller, paid homage to the centennial anniversary of his city by erecting a homemade Statue of Liberty. La Mona (The Doll) appeared from one day to the next from within Colonia Libertad, one of Tijuana's oldest informal, favela-like communities. Her arms reaching for the sky, La Mona invokes the irony of liberty in this context, but she also stands for the political role of women in the city.

La Mona was not only a monument to Armando Muñoz's city; he wanted to live inside her. So La Mona became a permanent expansion to his house, sheltering an additional bedroom, bathroom, and small kitchenette. Just as the Situationists imagined, the ultimate avant-garde action occurs the moment that an average citizen is able to appropriate the spaces and the materials of the city.

Spontaneous gestures such as the Horse and the Doll allow us to glimpse the subjective and collective struggles of a community locked into conflicts that are being played out in the border zones: the most derelict and unexpected places have the potential to become sites for light occupations that challenge the massive colonization of traditional urbanism. For San Diego as well as Tijuana, the Horse and the Doll have become political symbols that remind us of the opportunities opened up by an insurgent, flexible urbanism that insinuates itself into the most rigid contexts.

Tour 3 *North to South: Disposable Housing*

Jose Peralta, a Tijuana speculator, travels to San Diego to buy up little bungalows that have been slated for demolition to make space for new condominium projects. The little houses are loaded onto trailers and prepared to travel to Tijuana, where they will have to clear customs before making their journey south. For days, one can see houses, just like cars and pedestrians, waiting in line to cross the border. Finally the houses enter into Tijuana and are mounted on one-story metal frames that leave an empty space at the street level to accommodate future uses. These houses and the space of opportunity lying beneath them are emblematic not only of an architecture of juxtaposition and ambiguity generated at the border but become the manifestos of a temporal urbanism that is open to adaptability and transformation.

One city profits from the material that the other one wastes. Tijuana recycles the leftover buildings of San Diego, recombining them in fresh scenarios, creating countless new opportunities.

Tour 4 *South to North: Illegal Zoning*

Increasing waves of immigrants from Latin America have had a major impact on the urbanism of American cities. Already Los Angeles, for example, is home to the second largest concentration of former Latin American nationals outside the capitals of their respective countries of origin, Mexico, Guatemala, El Salvador, and other countries. Current demographic studies have predicted that Latin Americans will comprise the majority of California's population within the next decade. As people travel north in search of new opportunities, they inevitably alter and transform the fabric of certain neighborhoods in cities like Los Angeles and San Diego. The immigrants bring with them their socio-cultural attitudes and sensibilities regarding the use of domestic and public space as well as the natural landscape. In these neighborhoods, multi-generational households of extended families shape their own programs of use, taking charge of their own mini-economies in order to maintain standards for the household. Their actions generate illegal, non-conforming uses and high densities that reshape the fabric of the residential neighborhoods where they settle. Alleys, setbacks, driveways, and other wasted infrastructures and leftover spaces are appropriated and utilized as communities see fit.

Such temporal, informal economies and accompanying patterns of density promoted by waves of immigrant communities have been impacting the inner city neighborhoods of many American cities during the last decades. They have fundamentally altered what was the first ring of Levittown-type sub-urbanization of the 1950s, transforming the homogeneity of these early subdivisions into more complex networks of socio-cultural and economic relationships. Obviously, it is in these neighborhoods that we find most of the working "diasporas," the "service communities" that support the newly glamorous projects of re-development currently in train in many downtowns across the US. By critically observing how these temporal and contingent urbanisms have contaminated the rigidity of zoning within older fabrics, allowing alternative modes of sociability and density, perhaps we can anticipate how the one-dimensionality of the MacMansions now sprawling in the third, fourth, and fifth rings of sub-urbanization will be retrofitted with difference in the next five decades.

Tour 5 *South not like North: Two Urbanisms*

At no other political juncture in the world does one find one of the wealthiest housing subdivisions in the United States only 20 minutes away from some of the poorest settlements in Latin America.

1. Urbanism of Sameness: Beige Architectures

As the bulldozers of private developers (subsidized by public infrastructure) obsessively flatten the landscape of San Diego's natural network of canyons into a vast plain of tract subdivisions and housing pads, the question of the relationship between civic identity and landscape, and thus between development and land-use, is re-opened. In this context, the most emblematic image of identity is the fingerprint, whose unique patterns resemble topographic contours. Through this analogy, we can speculate that topography is the physical manifestation of identity since there are never two topographic conditions that are precisely the same. If we obliterate topography, then we are canceling identity. The massive and expensive eradication of topography in the periphery of San Diego for the purpose of creating the one-dimensional infrastructure that can support the (ever-cheaper) construction of housing projects by private developers not only neutralizes the character of the ground and erases its political, historical, and cultural meanings, but also imprints on it, as Mike Davis has pointed out, an ecology of fear that ultimately flattens, along its path, any sense of political will and social responsibility. Ultimately, San Diego's sprawl is the emblem of an urbanism characterized by "distance separation," yielding a beige architecture of conformity and homogeneity that eradicates history and hides conflict.

2. Urbanism of Juxtaposition: Differential Architectures

Contrary to San Diego, Tijuana's intensive urbanism of "distance mitigation" is emblematic of how this city's informal communities are growing faster than the urban cores they surround, creating a different set of rules for development and blurring distinctions between the urban, suburban, and rural. These start-up settlements gradually evolve—or violently explode—out of conditions of social emergency, and are defined by the negotiation of territorial boundaries, the ingenious recycling of materials, and human resourcefulness.

Hundreds of dwellers, called "parachuters," invade, en masse, large public, (sometimes private) vacant properties. As these urban guerillas parachute into the hills of Tijuana's edges, they are organized and choreographed by what are commonly called "urban pirates." Armed with

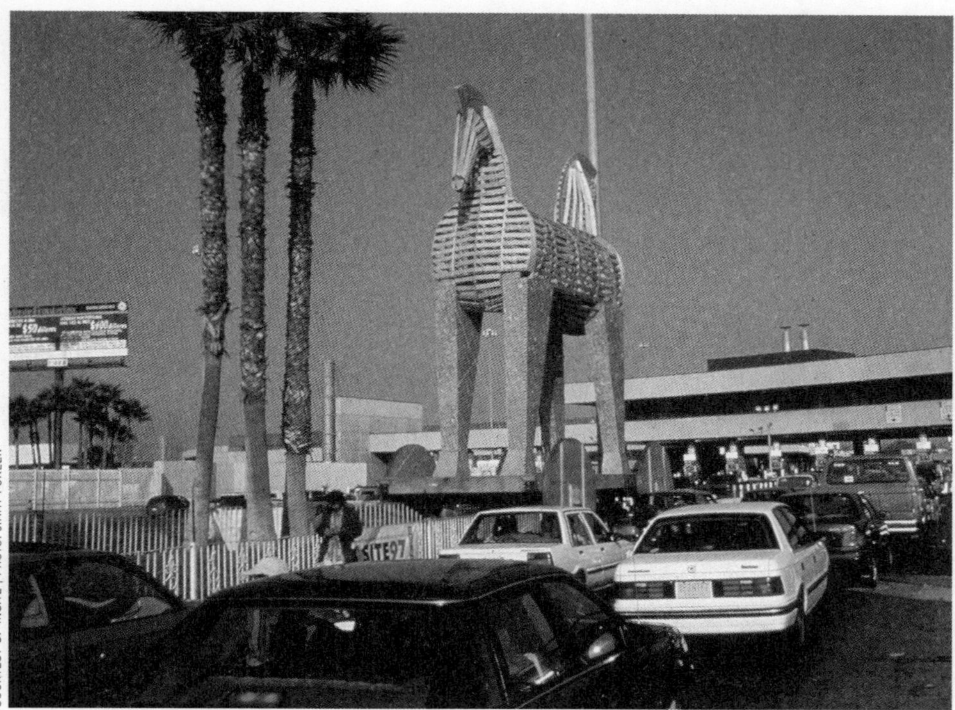

COURTESY OF INSITE | PHOTO: JIMMY FUKLER

Marcos Ramírez ERRE
Toy an Horse, 1997
12' x 33' x 29',
wood and metal hardware
Installation View
inSITE97

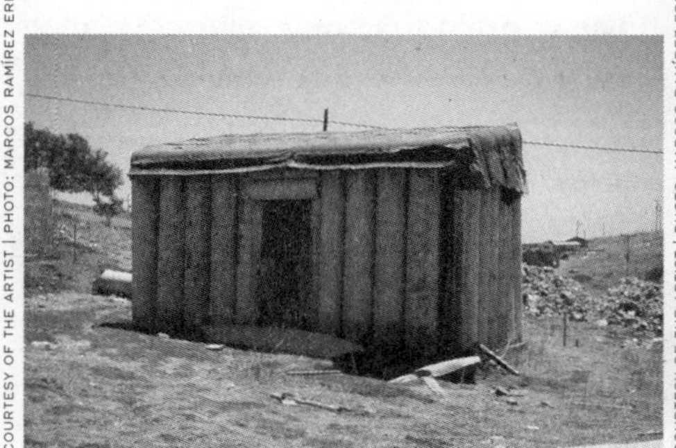

COURTESY OF THE ARTIST | PHOTO: MARCOS RAMÍREZ ERRE

House of Tubes, 2002

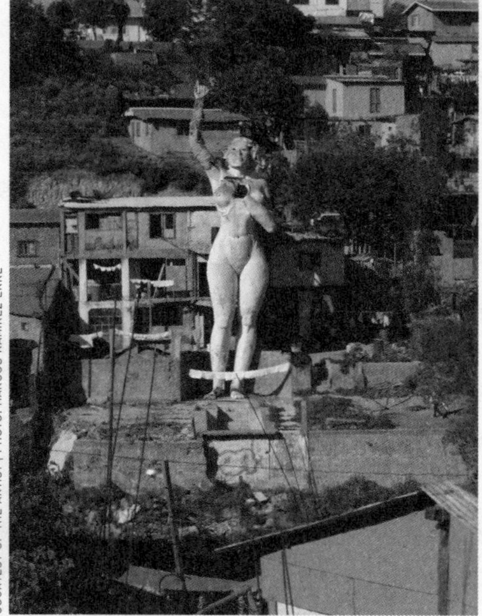

COURTESY OF THE ARTIST | PHOTO: MARCOS RAMÍREZ ERRE

La Mona, 2004

cellular phones, these characters are the community activists in charge of organizing the first deployment of people on these empty sites and their post-invasion struggle to request services from the local municipality. Through improvisational tactics of construction and distribution of goods and ad hoc services, a process of assembly begins by recycling the systems and materials from San Diego's urban debris. Garage doors make walls; rubber tires are cut and dismantled into folded loops that are clipped in an eight-shape and interlocked, creating a system that threads a more stable retaining wall; wooden crates form the armatures for other imported surfaces, such as abandoned refrigerator doors, etc. After months of organic construction, the neighborhood begins to request services from the city. In other words, inhabitation happens first and infrastructure follows. The city sends trucks to deliver water at certain locations (one of the first infrastructural elements to be implemented is a water tank on top of some dwellings). Electricity follows as the city sends one official line, expecting the community to "borrow" the rest via a series of illegal clippings called "diablitos" (little devils). These sites are made by stitching together such multiple internal and external situations simultaneously. The interiors of the resultant dwellings become their exteriors, expressive of their domestic histories and their pragmatic evolution.

Tour 6 *South Imports North: Tijuana's Mini Gated Communities*

As Tijuana grows eastward and is seduced by the style and glamour of the master-planned, gated communities of the US, it finds itself building its own versions of the San Diego dream: miniaturized replicas of typical suburban Southern California tract homes, paradoxically imported into Tijuana to provide social housing. Thousands of tiny tract homes are now scattered around the periphery of Tijuana, creating a vast landscape of homogeneity and division quite at odds with TJ's prevailing heterogeneous and organic metropolitan condition. These diminutive dwellings come equipped with all the clichés and conventions of what they simulate: manicured landscaping, gate houses, model units, banners and flags, mini-set backs, front and back yards.

This is the new social housing subsidized by the Mexican federal government, courtesy of private developers and speculators. Whereas the gated communities of San Diego remain closed systems due to stringent zoning that prohibits any kind of formal alteration or programmatic juxtaposition, the housing tracts of Tijuana quickly submit to transformation by their occupants who are little hindered by comparatively permissive zoning regulations. The ways in which occupants customize their tract houses—filling-in setbacks, occupying front and back yards as well as garages with more construction and overlapping programs—mirror the strategies common to older informal communities of the city rather than the idealized suburban dream house.

The tactics of encroachment taken up by resourceful Tijuana residents may prefigure the fate of urban densification in many cities around the world, where redevelopment has been driven by privatization, homogenization, and style. If the gated residential communities on both sides of the San Diego/Tijuana border derive from a common recipe, the former insists on foreclosing the possibility of change over time, while the latter remains open to unpredictable futures. The gated communities of San Diego, which will soon stand in the shadow of the newly-designed border checkpoint, exemplify the dominant paradigm for a post-9/11 fortified city where public life, public space, and public institutions and transportation hubs are increasingly barricaded against complexity and contradiction. The imitation tract housing developments in Tijuana, on the other hand, are inspiring and liberating in their search for strategies of improvisation, layering, juxtaposition, and negotiation of a territory conceived as an operative and flexible horizon.

Tour 7 *South Only: Houses of Desire*
A day in the life of Colonia Libertad (Freedom Neighborhood) in Tijuana

"Here, unlike any other place, dreams have broken steps as if they were old ladders."

House 1

José Hernández builds a house. He has wrapped it with pieces of cardboard that he picked up from the trash at the "curios" market where he works. It was there he was also able to find other left over "stuff" to build the rest of his walls. Approximately 40 pallet racks that his neighbor's boss sold him after retrieving a shipment of clay figurines from

Guadalajara that a truck driver had mysteriously abandoned without getting paid. José got a couple of blue canvases from the flea market that comes to his neighborhood every Tuesday and used them to fabricate a temporary roof. The shade of blue he chose was a bit stronger than the light sky-blue that he likes so much, but the canvas is useful anyway, in order to stop the water-leak that has been dripping into the space that he is currently using as kitchen.

At the house's entrance there is a nice patterned cotton curtain that, from the inside, hides a crooked door that doesn't close all the way—though it allows he and his wife to sleep peacefully at night as it can be connected to a wooden post with a chain. José was also able to pay monthly installments to his neighborhood's hardware store for a couple of French windows, the ones that have multiple mullions, so if the window breaks, he doesn't have to replace the whole thing, just the broken pane. For furniture, José has a strange mixture of styles and colors, which he wants to edit further, immediately after taking care of the most pressing necessities. It is useless, he says in order to console himself, to have a strong, uniform array of furniture when you don't have an appropriate floor surface. José's floor is made of compacted dirt that he has to water constantly to avoid the dust cloud that makes everything dirty and his family feel suffocated.

But there is a refrigerator. José does not tolerate warm beer. Besides, his wife and two daughters need this appliance a lot more than he does. It is as indispensable to them as the $30 television set that José bought for his wife, Teresa, for their last wedding anniversary. The Hernández also own a battery-operated radio and a camping stove which works with a small gas cylinder, allowing them to cook for two weeks at a time. The rest of their household goods, clothing, appliances, utensils, dishes, blankets, and linens they find here and there, either by buying them or by receiving them as gifts. Not everything that they have is to their liking but everything is useful. They arrived at this spot just a few months ago, and in time they will save more money to finish painting their house. But this will only happen after they finish building a fence and a place for washing. In reality, however, it will not happen until they finally receive an official electrical supply that will supplant the service they have been stealing, like everyone else. Among their other priorities is to replace the parabolic dish that the wind took away the other night when it wouldn't stop raining. In retrospect, what all of this comes down to is that none of these desires will eventuate until their uncle, who is the leader of the neighborhood's liberal political party, fulfills his promise finally to give them the property title of the small lot where José and his family build their house every day.

House 2

Antonio Madrigal is constructing his house on a small lot that he found in Colonia Libertad. Since this is one of Tijuana's oldest neighborhoods it was very difficult to find a leftover lot. This is mainly because the only parcels remaining have been passed down from family to family, so unless one of these families is evicted or emigrates to the other side, little comes up. The lot that Antonio found is big enough, though a bit crooked, and has really great views. In addition, it came with a small wooden hut at the back that Antonio initially thought of demolishing, but for now is using as storage and later will turn into a guesthouse.

He eventually wants to build an average house and has saved $30,000.00 over the last five years by working in California. It has been very hard for Antonio to put that amount away by working in the shipyards of National City while at the same time paying for the lot and the used car he recently acquired. He is committed to continue the construction of his house now that he has finally laid out the foundation with the help of a construction worker who he recently met, along with a couple of assistants who offered to join in the effort. The house design is a mixture of styles. First and foremost, however, it aspired to the Californian style he copied from some magazines that his girlfriend (and future wife) Estella found at a beauty salon. She would have preferred to live on the other side but she is now resigned to Antonio's stubborn determination to build in Tijuana. Because of the rising prices of houses in the country next door, she persuaded her fiancé to build a miniature replica of a historic California bungalow. But she is determined that the new house will come with all the appropriate detailing, as there's nothing more annoying than being poor and having to show it. Antonio, on the other hand, wanted a simple, open house with ample space for the children that will arrive sooner or later, a two-car garage and a small salon or rec room so he can have fun with his buddies. It is, in fact, his friends who have advised him on minor design adjustments here and there, such as brick walls to retain the daytime heat, arches that reinforce the Spanish and Moorish inheritance, exterior stucco detailing with a lot of color, and wrought iron bars over the windows (these are always good to have because this neighborhood is still dangerous).

For the interior their wish list includes stucco detailing painted with oil paint, a king-size bed, a big armoir that can conceal their 48" TV and a fluffy rug. In the kitchen they want a ten-person dining table, walnut cabinets with granite tops, all the appliances colored beige and a parquet floor that matches the finish of the table. In the living room they would like a plain leather sofa, a coffee table with a glass top, an oriental rug and a few plastic plants to reinforce the fresh-n'cozy character of the dwelling. At least this is what Antonio wants. Estella wants even more, but for now they have only built the foundation and the few walls that the construction worker, a couple of assistants, and the $30,000 savings can provide. While Antonio builds his house he will continue working in the shipyards, he will marry Estella, and little by little, a fraction, or maybe even the entire house, will become a reality ... some day.

House 3

Carlos Roldan just finished building his house. In reality it is not the only one he owns. There are many. His family has been in this region for a long time. At one point, when he was a kid, his father had the vision to establish several businesses and acquire land since it was then so cheap it was almost given away for free. He now has access to the great fortune he inherited from his father as well as many lots in the city and a series of bars located in Tijuana's red zone. But, one day, tired of living in the neighborhood and the bad reputation that follows businesses like his, he decided to build a house in a more prestigious zone in order to be surrounded by the people that could give an extra shine to his shoes. The house is ready. It was built in record time. It is always good to count on a solid budget. The lots are big in that gated community and can become huge if one buys more than one parcel, as Carlos did. He hired one of the most prestigious architects in Tijuana—who had won many competitions, including for Tijuana's new cathedral, the addition to a cultural center, supermarkets, and the residences for many of the city's most important families. He studied in Mexico City and he writes art and architecture reviews in the cultural section of the official newspaper.

Carlos is planning a big party to inaugurate the house. One hundred guests will attend, not because the house will not accommodate more people, but because he wants people to feel comfortable, enjoying the facilities and amenities that he offers in a more intimate way. If people want to play tennis, there are three courts, two swimming pools for those who feel the desire to dive into the water and a gymnasium that, even though it might not sound like an appropriate context for a party, is always available for any occasion. On the edges of the main house and overlooking Tijuana's main canal, there are also a couple of guesthouses, each with very large chimneys and big bars filled with all kinds of wines and liquors. These areas of the house and the gardens that connect them are always a success with guests, but as the night goes on attention will shift to the bedrooms. The details of the house's decor are not that important, but everything, let's put it this way, is extremely expensive. Some of the decoration is done in good taste, some it is not. Well, what else can be said? Carlos is very satisfied. The party was a success and it seems that his social horizon is expanding every day. He is very interested in real estate and construction as areas for economic growth. So, it is certain that in the near future Carlos will continue managing bars and other construction projects.

Epilogue: Zero Urbanism: Zero Art?

It is paradoxical that the border's transformation in the last decades from porous to solid is the exact opposite of the recent shifts in contemporary architecture and artistic practices within the city, which have moved from solid to light. For the ethos of Tijuana urbanism has migrated from formalist, autonomous architectural projects, produced by the closed, self-referential disciplinarity of the last decades, that are indifferent to the politics and economics of land-use, to current operational strategies that interdisciplinary groups are putting into practice across the untapped resources found within diverse communities, jurisdictions, and institutions. These contemporary projects are searching, once more, for nomadic traditions of lightness and openness, less interested in objects of imposition and more in territorial tactics, engaging the boundaries that simultaneously delimit and blur the diverse socio-cultural geographies of contemporary life.

Inherent in this paradox is the vulnerability of contemporary urbanism's desire for revisiting the meaning of dynamic metropolitan landscapes such as the ones found in Latin American, Asian, and African cities, searching for new models of development based on layered programmatic intensities. Also vulnerable is contemporary architecture's quest for new formal expressions based on strategies of transformation and open-endedness, as well as current artistic practices that want to insert themselves into the problematic of the shifting cultural demographics and inter-human relational dynamics. Yet insofar as these notions are liberating, their achievement is put into question by discriminating social policies toward the "public" in many American cities, a condition that is radicalized at the border. If contemporary art, architecture, and urbanism do not enter the socio-political, economic, and cultural dimension of the territories they occupy, they are destined to continue being isolated formal events, perpetuating the idea of the city as a static repository of objects instead of revealing its potential as a dynamic field whose thickness is made of the complexity of its multiple forces and mutating histories and identities.

In other words, as architects and artists are once more reclaiming the city as the privileged site for investigation and experimentation, searching for possible models of sociability that are more inclusive and heterogeneous, it is doubtful whether these ideals can be achieved under the conditions that prevail at the beginning of the 21st century, as the post-9/11 city is incrementally defined by intensified layers of "security" against invisible threats. In this sense, we are reminded that the policies being rolled out by the department of Homeland Security may not be as benign as they seem. For in their blind desire to reinforce barriers, to lock out what is different and unpredictable, they of course run the risk of locking the door on the wrong side. It is at this juncture, in the context of this socio-cultural closure, that alternative urban and artistic practices must, once more, camouflage themselves in the shape of a Trojan horse.

Endpapers

This essay was first published on the occasion of "Facing the Music," curated by Allan Sekula for Gallery at REDCAT, Los Angeles, April 14–May 29, 2005. The exhibition included photographs by Anthony Hernandez and Karin Apollonia Müller; a digital installation by James Baker; and Billy Woodberry's DVD, The architect, the ants and the bees *(2005); as well as Sekula's 18-minute DVD* Gala *(2005), and slide projection piece,* Prayer for the Americans 3 (Disney Stockholders) *(1997/2005).* JCW

Facing the Music

Allan Sekula

... and the city was ringed with fire.

Six years ago, only the slab, "level zero," was visible. Beneath were layered ramp-linked floors of parking for jurors serving in the civil and criminal courts just across the street and down the hill. A grand escalator led upward to nothing but the glare of the California sun on horizontal concrete. The interrupted dream of a symphony hall, would, when realized, continue to offer its lower depths to the jury pool, dual-usage in a city where *parking is king*, and where the venerable buses of the County Sheriff deliver an unending parade of the accused to the bench, some making the journey for the third and last time.

Thus our exhibition's title offered gratefully to a metropolis whose boosters, planners, and architects often fail to notice, or chose deliberately to ignore, the sheer wealth of ironic juxtaposition on the city streets.

A young architect briefly charged with coming up with a new scheme for the amenities and shrubs along Grand Avenue brashly compared himself to Baron Haussmann, the redeveloper-in-chief of mid-19th century Paris. Hoping to stimulate the varied and richly satisfying nightlife so lacking in our city center but found in the renovated downtowns of lesser neighboring cities such as San Diego and Pasadena, the young planner suggested that the commercial development soon to be erected just to the east of the new symphony hall might appropriately host a House of Blues. Think of old delta bluesmen invited to serenade the condemned, passing on memories of the jailhouse and chain gang. The proposal is beyond the Depression-era ironies of *Sullivan's Travels*, beyond even the cynicism of its recent remake. No need now for Johnny Cash to bother taking the bus to Folsom Prison. Will the inmates, peering through the barred windows of the Sheriff's bus into the hard daylight, catch a fleeting glimpse of a *faux*-rustic delta juke joint cloned from its cousin on the Sunset Strip, clad in galvanized sheet metal? And beyond that, a strange luminous leviathan of brighter stuff?

At the end of the 1930s, the film critic Otis Ferguson likened Los Angeles to a Manhattan dispersed outward, its landmarks scattered at random from the Jersey Shore to Long Island. Looking eastward, we can visualize another sort of cognitive remapping. Imagine the Lincoln Center, the Museum of Modern Art, Saint Patrick's Cathedral, the Criminal Courts, City Hall, P.S.1, Julliard, Times Square, Canal Street, Chinatown, Grand Central Station, and the Tombs, all compressed by magical plate tectonics within the granite bedrock of the island into one dense, walk-able zone of a few square blocks. Except that nobody (nobody "middle-class," that is) is walking. That would be Manhattan on the model of downtown Los Angeles. In other words, the sort of downtown familiar to residents of smaller cities such as Columbus, Ohio: a modest "Midwestern" downtown—a Zenith on the Pacific.

So this was our task as artists, such as we hashed it out over a couple of dinners intermittently talking and listening to Thai Elvis, who may or may not have been lip-synching. A facelift for music: the dowager hall of the 1960s yields to the new starlet on the block in her shiny metallic gown. How do we face the facelift, and follow the real and imaginary lines outward along First Street and Grand Avenue?

Los Angeles is a city that defies the documentary genre: too protean, overly obsessed with fantastic schemes of what could be rather than confronting the concrete immediacy of the present or disturbing memories of the past. The automobile eliminates the pedestrian elbow-rubbing closeness so conducive to social observation. However, between 1930 and 1960 much of the vibrancy of Bunker Hill's densely populated working-class neighborhood life was, in fact, described in social realist works of art ranging from the fiction of John Fante and paintings of Millard Sheets, to the photographs of Leonard Nadel and films of Kent McKenzie. So the Walt Disney Concert Hall, like Dodger Stadium, is an amnesiac monument erected above a forgotten tomb, urban social memory cut short by eviction.

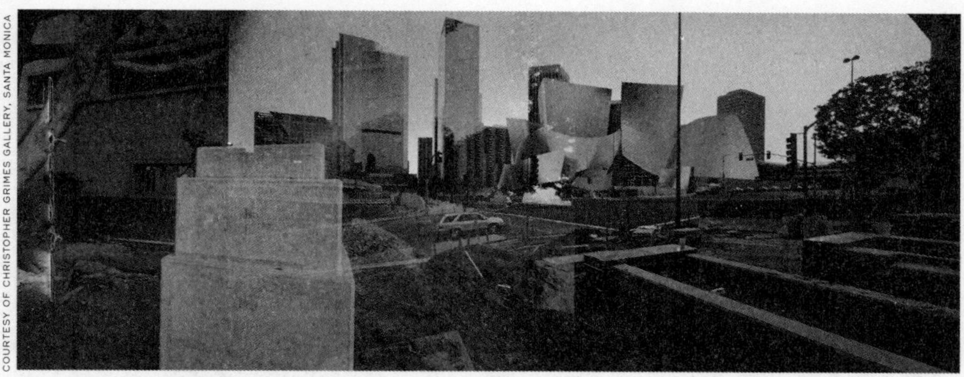

COURTESY OF CHRISTOPHER GRIMES GALLERY, SANTA MONICA

Alan Sekula
Prayer for the Americans 4, 2003/2005
Chromogenic print, 111-3/4 × 49 inches
Edition 1/5

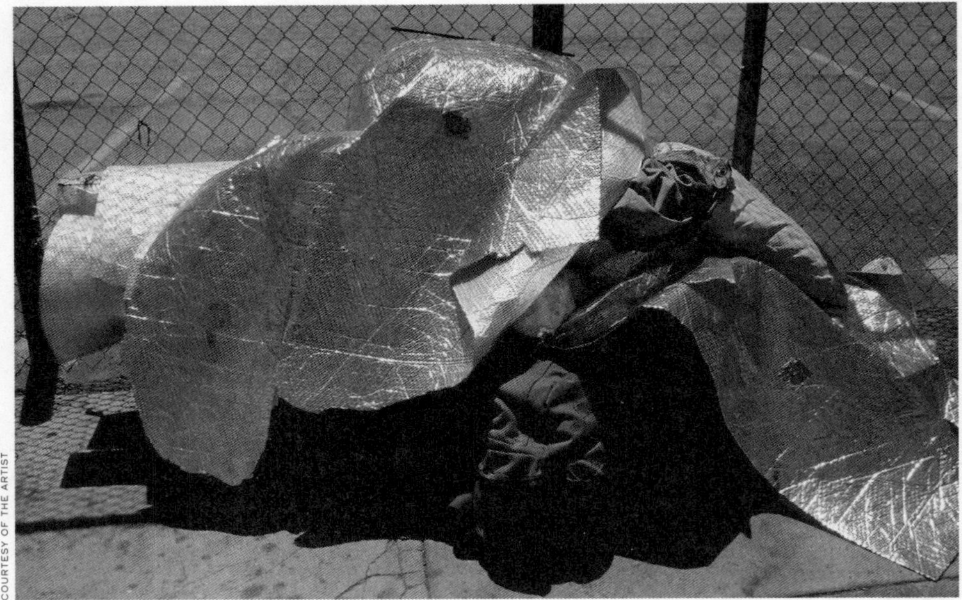
COURTESY OF THE ARTIST

James Baker
Untitled, 2005
Digital installation

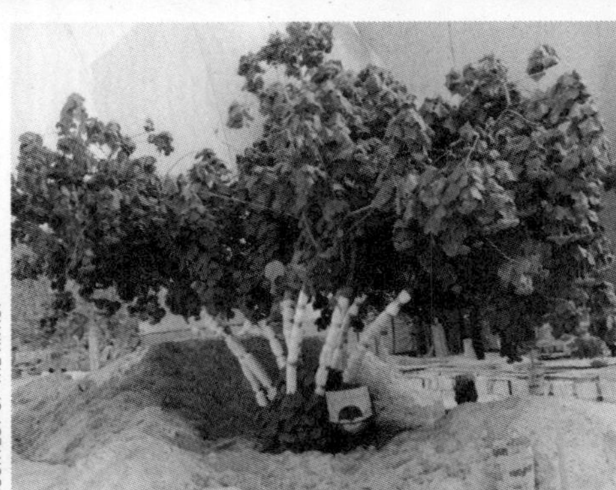
COURTESY OF THE ARTIST

Karin Apollonia Müller
From *Tree Series*, 2005
Type C Print, 40 x 50 inches

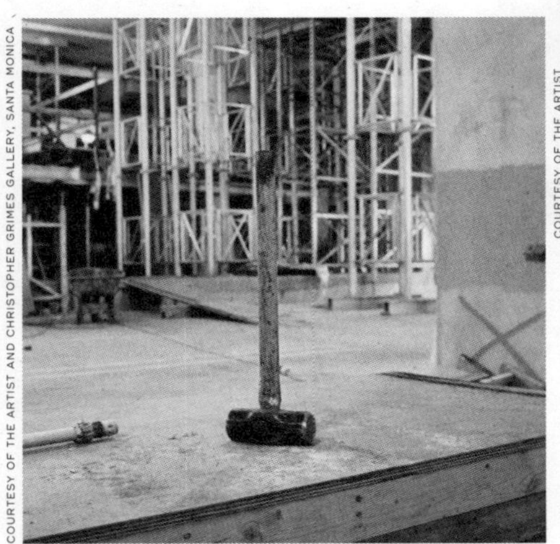
COURTESY OF THE ARTIST AND CHRISTOPHER GRIMES GALLERY, SANTA MONICA

Anthony Hernandez
***Disney #1*, 2002–2003**
Type C Print, 40 x 40 inches,
Edition of 7

After a slow start with the Bunker Hill demolitions of the 1960s, Grand has finally become the avenue of culture and official spirituality, replete with what used to be called "ideology," stretching from Arata Isozaki's Museum of Contemporary Art, set like a little jade and ruby jewel-box within Arthur Erickson's California Plaza, the latter a hulking space offering regrettably only occasional free concerts of Sufi *kawali* music, drawing Pakistani and Muslim freethinkers from miles around, on to Raphael Moneo's Cathedral, a veritable fortress for clerical obfuscation, and beyond that, across the freeway, to the site of a new high school of performing arts, brainchild of philanthropist and suburban real estate developer Eli Broad, to be designed by the Vienna firm of Coop Himmelblau. So, even if a new house of music fails to attract youthful elites to the delights of the new downtown, there will be a plentiful reserve army of young musicians ready to sing or wait tables for their supper. As Bertolt Brecht said of Hollywood, it could be heaven and it could be hell.

Meanwhile, our intrepid Master and Commander, Frank Gehry, navigates his East Indiaman up the dry riverbed from the third largest harbor in the world, mooring it to the bollards of the new "city center." (Gehry acknowledges inspiration from the billowing sails of seventeenth century Dutch maritime painting, but has anyone noticed his debt to one of the most eccentric and wonderful projects of Louis Kahn, a metal-clad concert barge?) Here it looms, bow forward, a floating "living room" for the metropolis, modestly hoping to blend in and become comfortable like a converted cargo barge on the Prinsengracht in Amsterdam.

But where exactly is the bollard, the mooring post, for this phantom of maritime domesticity, the elder sister of Bilbao's pirate ship of global culture? Could it have been the bronze portrait bust of Abraham Lincoln, who not so long ago confronted jurors and lawyers and bailiffs alike with a melancholic stare as they crossed First Street, in what I came to appreciate as my private local version of *Mr. Smith Goes to Washington*? But, sadly Abe has been evicted from his pedestal, rotated 90 degrees toward the dowager Music Center, shifted back to a hidden nook behind a planter, keeping a low profile like an immigrant without papers under the shady green canopy of two elderly but sturdy ficus trees.

Maybe the trees, then? Those trees, at least, have been allowed to survive the slaughter of their nearby relatives, a crime recorded with topographic precision in an excellent photograph made by Karin Apollonia

Müller. Her *Tree Series* (2003–2005) also follows the risky cross-town transplanting—the very life and death of migratory trees—in a backstage story of fable-like sadness about the synesthetic orchestration of a "symphony in bloom."

First Street, by contrast, languishes in the reflected heat and light. Here is the axis of government and of what was—until the 1960s—the local king-making fusion of government and big business: the *Los Angeles Times*. Its Art Deco entrance still displays Harry Chandler's legendary union-busting motto: "True Industrial Freedom." Across the street, the courthouses have fallen into a state of functioning decrepitude as they continue to process record numbers of cases. It appears that the County Law Library, a public resource of inestimable value in a society in which the narrowing road to social justice is still paved with the right to sue, may well be closed in the near future.

The post-New Deal *gravitas* of the California of Earl Warren and Edmund Brown is faded and unappreciated as civic architecture. Even conservative downtown real-estate boosters who advocate a minimal state apparatus, dedicated only to war and policing, are unwilling to see new police headquarters on their side of the street, as if any inviting target for protestors and enemy commandos will drive down property values. And our concert-hall architect's essential modesty is now confirmed by Thom Mayne's immense new metallic Juggernaut dedicated to the only other government agency that seems to matter anymore, the California Department of Transportation, a façade depicting in minimalist relief a freeway miraculous for its post-apocalyptic lack of traffic density. (And, miracle of miracles, there seem to be almost as many buses as cars.) Presuming the real-estate bubble doesn't burst, this imposing new building will, in its turn, also be rendered cute and toy-like alongside the commercial skyscrapers planned for First Street.

Anthony Hernandez gives us another extended reading of First Street, one that crosses the Harbor Freeway to the west and the Los Angeles River to the east. Eastward, he prowls the abandoned living rooms of the semi-demolished Aliso Village public housing project where he spent his early childhood, and westward, he trespasses amidst the folly of the Belmont Learning Center—the most expensive high school in American history—abandoned and half-demolished before occupancy because no one thought to test the subsoil for methane gas and earthquake faults. Two photographs by Hernandez, one from Belmont and one from Disney Hall, show construction in or out of progress in which Gehry's baroque architectural distinction is abolished by stubborn attention to the rectilinearity of ordinary walls and corridors. The senior art critic of the *Los Angeles Times* has suggested that one would be hard-pressed to find a bad photograph of Disney Hall, given the building's seductive beauty, which offers a kind of ready-made artfulness to minor artists, amateurs, and tourist snap-shooters. Hernandez's pictures slyly evade this trap, by exploring only an uncanny kinship with uncelebrated structures, and with a pictorial modernism free from baroque aspirations. His sledgehammer pictured in *Disney #1* (2002–2003) is as easily used for demolition as it is for driving steel wedges into place.

In *The architect, the ants and the bees* (2005), Billy Woodberry has devoted himself to a "city symphony" film that describes, in a series of short lyrical episodes, the laborious day-by-day making of this very unusual and demanding building. Disney Hall was showcase architecture, a union job with very stringent safety standards, unlike the accident-plagued subway built in the 1990s. So these proud aristocrats of labor know that despite their skill, work is good and life relatively secure only as long as the job lasts. Woodberry gives us a strong feeling for the temporal duration, rhythms, and dangers of work, relentlessly following the structure as it rises up out of the slab, unfolds its skeleton, and takes on its brilliant obscuring skin, not by itself, but with a little help from its hardworking friends. His film is the materialized memory of the building's coming-into-being, and for this reason more hauntingly "site-specific" than anything else in the exhibition.

James Baker's cinema-display sequence of photographs has the disarming slickness of a corporate media presentation, but the deadpan pacing, the wordlessness, and the content is all wrong. Disney Hall is embarrassingly close to zones of manufactured fantasy and downwardly-mobile dereliction. He takes us downhill toward the river, where rubber-gloved film crews—those other Los Angeles aristocrats of labor—and the homeless mingle in a strange informal economy at the edges of the shoot. More than any of us, he has explored the complicated social lives of the largest population that can claim to reside downtown, and for whom the city's new "living room" would seem to be ready-made.

Building a Better School: A Corrective Re-thinking of the Concepts

Meg Cranston

In the later 1980s and 1990s there were countless articles about the importance of the art schools in Southern California. The tone of many of them was faint astonishment. Writers, generally from New York or Europe, were surprised at how many well-known artists were teaching in Los Angeles art schools and how frequently those famous artists begot even more famous ones. They pondered the unfathomable mystery of how art might bloom in the desert. It would be hard to name an academic phenomenon that was more closely watched by the mainstream press.

All that has cooled off a bit. While the same schools are still full of very good and important artists and they still produce a regular batch of reliably significant young artists … they just aren't news any more. The schools have become institutions directed more by the long-range plans of administrators than the innovations of the faculty. The Los Angeles art school phenomenon is now a well-known formula and the schools have become virtually indistinguishable. For that reason I believe the time has come for a corrective rethinking of the fundamental concepts.

I will propose a general reducing plan for existing schools and then sketch how an entirely new one might look in practice. As I see it, that school will be both cheaper … and less helpful.

fundamental concept: build buildings for art
corrective re-thinking: stop building buildings for art

It may be too much to say that new buildings always drain the energy of an art school though I challenge anyone to prove they increase it.

I am not convinced that art schools need a building, but if they do have one it should be as efficient as possible. Large landscaped areas between buildings function mainly to increase the travel time of the simplest activities like getting a cup of coffee. Unalterable garden settings can be nice but not very useful for an artist. Dirt lots are much more useful and efficient than landscaping. Schools need lots of dirt lots.

The best room I ever taught in was located in a peculiar art school tenement. The classrooms and the library were on ground level and students lived in rooms on the floors above. The room had peeling linoleum mended with duct tape, an inexplicable stage, a green piano, a flagpole and scattered office desks. Those dreary things became props for many discussions including my famous "understanding minimalism in five seconds" demonstration, but the real secret of the room's success was that the place had fantastic flow. It was situated equidistant from the outside smoking area, the coffee vending machine and the toilets. Students with a room upstairs got an extra bonus. They could wake up 15 minutes before class, and have time to go to the toilet, get a coffee, have a cigarette and get to class on time. Some would arrive in their pajamas.

That building was not built. It grew around need.

fundamental concept: get rid of old couches
corrective re-thinking: have old couches

Old couches are highly contested. Maintenance people hate them. Administrators see them as a potential for a law suit (resting students are seen as dangerous) and people scamper by them on their campus tour. The truth is however, old couches serve an important practical and pedagogical function. The usually exhausted commuter art student often needs to cat nap. The distances in Los Angeles make going home usually impossible.

Old couches would help "time management." Pedagogically old couches and in days gone by big ashtrays shift the power relations between students and faculty in ways that are useful. Sitting on the couch with a student is a subtle form of initiation—a sign they are moving from student to artist. For example I would never sit on the couch with a first year student—couch sitting is for advanced students. Art schools must preserve the metaphor of the couch!

fundamental concept: schools should help students in any way they can
corrective re-thinking: care less

Old couches aside, students don't go to art school to be comfortable. They go to art school because they want to be artists and live the art life. They want something more interesting and simulating than ordinary life. They want adventure. Administrators typically and wrongheadedly believe that students need and want help because students are constantly complaining and asking for help. All that griping is just fearful backsliding into ordinary life. If you help them, they slide even further. Misery and confusion are necessary. Administrators believe students should be told clearly (in type-written form) what is expected of them. They should know how they will be graded and be permitted all sorts of redress if things don't go their way. That's all wrong.

I worked in a bar for years. We had a motto: Give them the worst and they'll come back for more. We learned through a process of trial and error that bar customers like action. They like something to chafe against. Because no one was willing to be the real bar manager, we regularly ran out of common items like beer and ice. The customer's initial annoyance would segue either into litigious rage or lively ingenuity. We would ignore the rager and let the rest use their imaginations. What if you mix Kahlua and Crème de Menthe? When they finally got a drink (i.e., warm gin in a plastic glass), they felt they had really accomplished something. Similarly we made it a strict policy never to clean the ashtrays. We would let them overflow until a customer plucked up the courage to grab a rag and do it themselves. It made them feel at home and cleaved them to us in just that way. That bar with no business plan, no

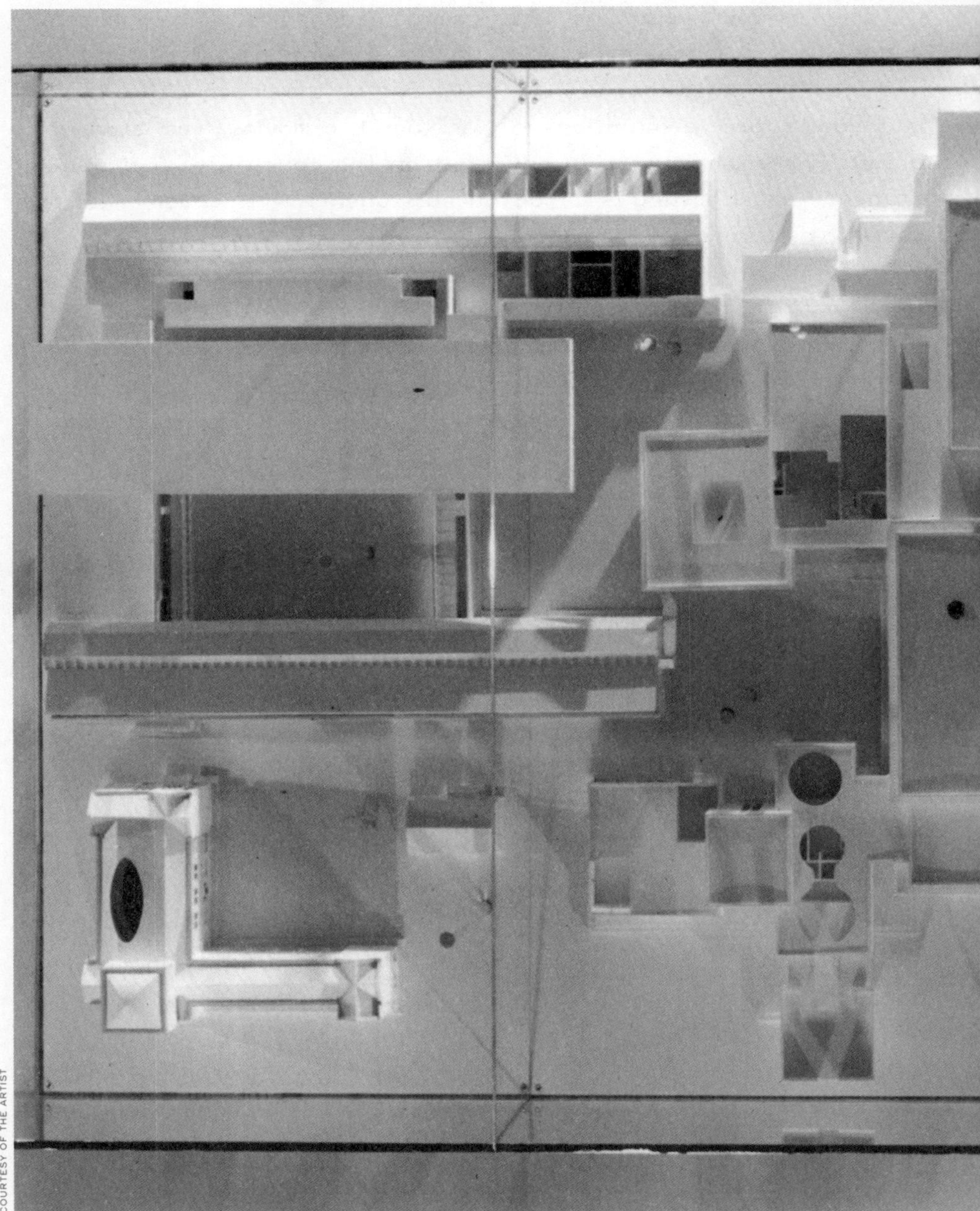

COURTESY OF THE ARTIST

Mike Kelley
Educational Complex, 1995
acrylic, latex, foamcore, fiberglass, wood
Collection Whitney Museum of American Art

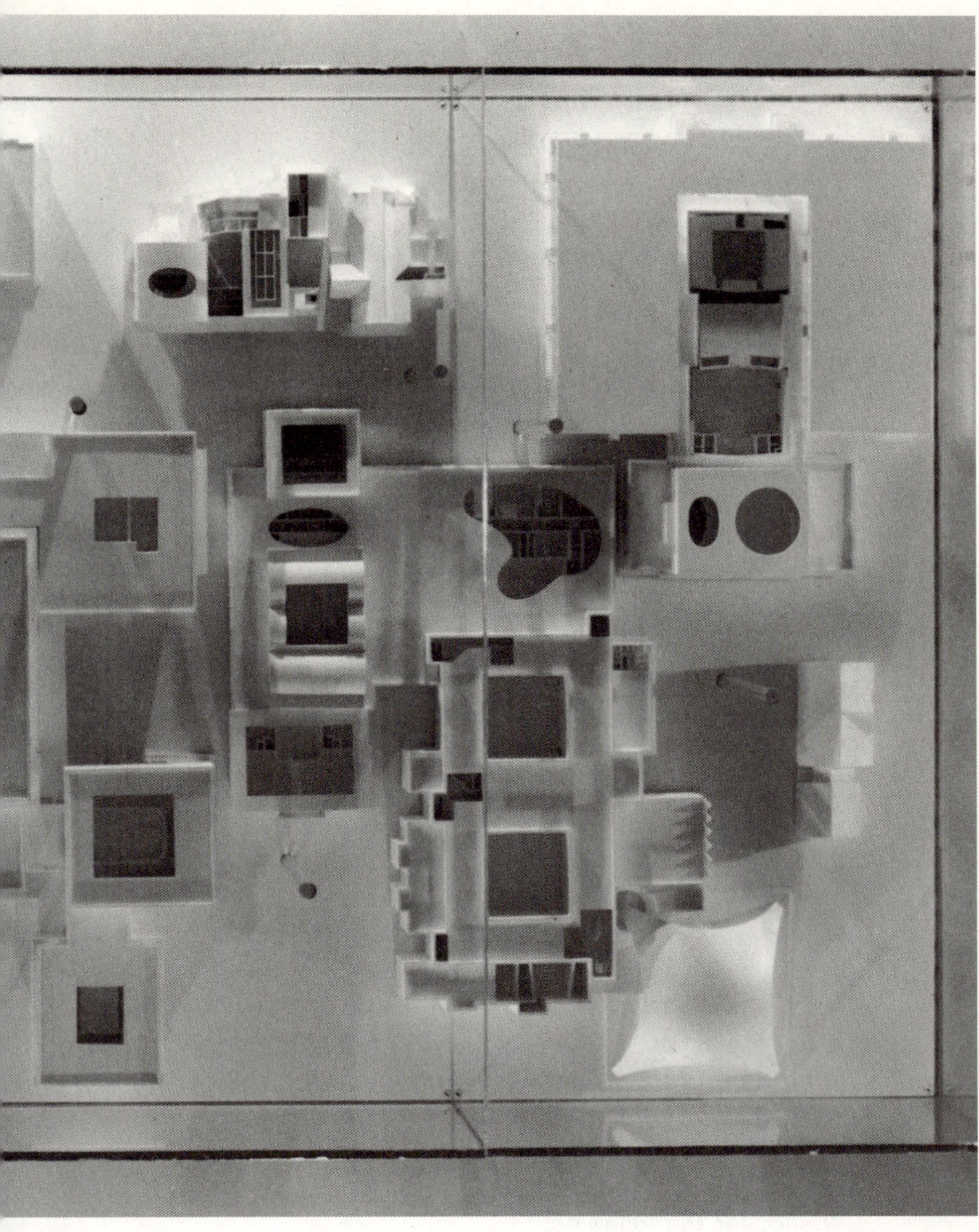

organization and armed only with a firm commitment to customer self-reliance is thriving.

Art schools should understand the wisdom of such an approach. fundamental concept: a great facility makes a great school—give students a lot of things.

corrective re-thinking: don't give the students any equipment

Typically, schools attempt to provide everything the student needs and indeed purchase things in anticipation of need. Schools "brand" themselves as having a state-of-the-art facility. That may or may not attract students but it does nothing for art.

Artists need to own the necessary tools to work independently. If they need a computer/camera/drill they should find a way to get one. If those tools are beyond their means they should reexamine their dependence on things they can't afford. Art school should be a process of outfitting your toolbox. Part of the reason so many students become painters after graduation is because painters always own the means of production. Even the worst painter would never use a borrowed brush.

* * *

Based on the principles described above, the following is my proposal for a new art school. It is a model for a graduate program. Since this model is for only 12 students and there are a thousand or more prospective graduate students trying to get into LA area schools, lots of people can get in on this. Ideally there would be many, many schools functioning around the region, each operating according to the particular principles of the founder and the participants.

I suggest the following:
Alert potential students that you are starting an art school
Designate a meeting date (i.e., every Monday) and place
(i.e., your backyard/studio)

Have students supply their own table and chair
(two five-gallon buckets are perfect)
Tell the students to buy and read the books you select.
Do not supply photocopies
Tell every student to get a library card
Meet every week for six hours
Provide: 2 1/2 hours of critique, 1 hour lunch, 2 1/2 hours
new information, then some books and films for group use

Students will complain about the lack of workspace and the total lack of facilities. Do nothing. This is an important lesson. Remember, the sooner the student gathers his/her own tools and finds an adequate work situation the better. Teach them self-reliance.

At the end of the course, talk will brew about having a student show. Again, don't assist. There are countless places dedicated to showing emerging artists. If they can't mange to hustle one of them into giving them a show they're hopeless, and you can't save them. Also, if they can't think of anything more original than having a gallery show they are totally hopeless. Wish them well with a hearty handshake.

Other rules:
No syllabus
No paperwork, no memos, no emails, no attendance sheets,
no faculty evaluation forms
No course catalog, no application (cash only)

BUDGET
Tuition: $500 per semester x 12 students = $6000
Faculty salary: $6000

Interested parties can contact me. Naturally, I won't tell
you how.

Theater of the Repressed ... or ... All I Got Was This Lousy MFA

Malik Gaines

On a first day of class, I ask the gathered art undergrads what media they like to work in. Among the budding painters and photographers and conceptual collagists of image and text, several say they are part of collaborative band/performance groups. It seems that the number of students who want to work in some medium that is described using a slash is now significant, and that hybrids of performance have become regular elements of New Genres programs. But are institutions really prepared for this hybridity?

Working in the interdiscipline is, as President Bush fondly describes his own job, "hard." I take, for example, the recent experience of finding a new studio for my own collaborative band/performance group, My Barbarian. There are spaces around town for bands: warehouses carved into sweaty little soundproofed rooms with whiney rock blaring in the hallways. There are artist's studio spaces, which have plenty of light and paper-thin walls and other artists to disturb with our loud drums and vigorous vocals. Since we need a combination of the two kinds of space, our task has been to convert one halfway into the other. This requires tricky explanations to landlords and results in general confusion regarding the question of artists making music, not to mention the money it takes to renovate real-estate. Space is so thoroughly codified that the actual physical place to do interdisciplinary work must be created each time anew.

And where do we present this work? My Barbarian's particular mix began in rock venues and has moved through galleries and theaters. Our new college radio-style record label likes us to play at grungy clubs. Here one deals with sound-guys who are pre-set for four fellows with guitars. You arrive, throw your stuff on the stage, and make your neo-punk gesture—between two other bands. The promoter of the night gives you a few bucks and a couple of free drinks, and then, if you are a real band, you hit the road for your next destination: San Diego, Omaha, Chapel Hill. In theaters, where several of my group began working, things can be much more "professional." One is given time to set the stage and angle the lights, and performers are thought of as deserving some remuneration. The audience sits attentively in their seats, but who are they? An eight-week run, in the theater tradition, brings out the venue's regular patrons who may not be prepared for anything more experimental than Our Town. Gallery and museum audiences are often hoping against hope to be surprised, and their directors can be supportive of unusual combinations of form, but the spaces themselves are acoustically challenged white cubes with no amplification systems and lights that are only good for paintings, hardly suitable for rhythmic polyphony or intimate narrative moments. Our task as artists, strangely like that of colonized subjects, is to continually redefine ourselves against our setting, using the limitations of our spaces' hegemonies as our structure.

How then do we make a living? Like most artists, we find other individual ways. As a group, the avenues are few (and narrow). Bands are meant to become pop sensations, artists are meant to sell commodities to collectors, and theater artists find niches within their institutions. Even private funding sources depend on categorization in order to function. One rare performance-based grant I've got my eye on asks if the applicants do "Experimental Music Performance" (I picture a naked woman hitting an amplified ice-cube with a spoon), "Performance Art/Theater" (Catherine Sullivan perhaps?), or "Music Theater" (enter trained Juilliard singers with the new Avenue Q). Once you fall between the cracks, things become very messy.

We have the 20th century to blame for this mess. The effects of its many avant-garde movements on today's work are difficult to assess, since it appears their great success was in asserting total failure: of form, of materials, of bourgeois expectation, of universal standards for quality, of applicability. From the upsets of early 20th-century Fauvism to the radical reversals of Dada, the social engineering of Russian Constructivism or the German Bauhaus, the self-conscious retorts of absurdist theater or the reductions of atonal music, Minimalist sculpture, or modern dance, to the maddening surrenders of Pop, art has been all about disintegration. When Ortega y Gasset called for a consideration of the window through which we see the view rather than the view itself, when Marcel Duchamp dismissed "retinal art,"[1] when Clement Greenberg wrote that "if the abstract is indeed impoverishing, then such impoverishment has now become necessary to important art,"[2] they were each calling, in different voices, for the dismissal of Aristotelian unities, Renaissance chiaroscuros, and Kantian sublimes—of all transcendent illusion. Everything suddenly is what it is.

And what it is, is not always pretty. It becomes impossible in this context to ignore the setting for Western art production, which since modern times has been the alienated urban space in which an intellectual elite does a dance of willing deception with its benefaction, subject to the violence of capitalism (even in communist contexts, which, as Guy Debord described them, simply implemented a state of "bureaucratic" capitalism;[3] it is said that the costly and elaborate state-supported storming of the Winter Palace in Sergei Eisentsein's *October* [1927] enacted for the sake of political realism, brought more damage to the building than was done during the actual Russian Revolution). Such folly! Though avant-garde art movements gave us much to ponder, and extend art's value into our disjoined present by creating a temporal trajectory by which artists may continually reinvent the last reinventions, Marinetti's declared goal of destroying "Art with a capital A,"[4] a goal which permutated throughout our parenting century, has made it increasingly difficult to defend art as a distinct discipline replete with its own private access to aesthetic value and historical agency.

Perhaps knowing what forces were being set in motion, artists of the bygone avant-garde regularly sought pathways out of their strict disciplines. Though audiences at the time were apparently outraged, I imagine the ballet *Parade* to be one of the finer moments of 1917. Erik Satie's score, which included parts for typewriter and the like, was set to Jean Cocteau's text, while Pablo Picasso provided ludicrously oversized costumes, and Léonide Massine invented the movement. While the

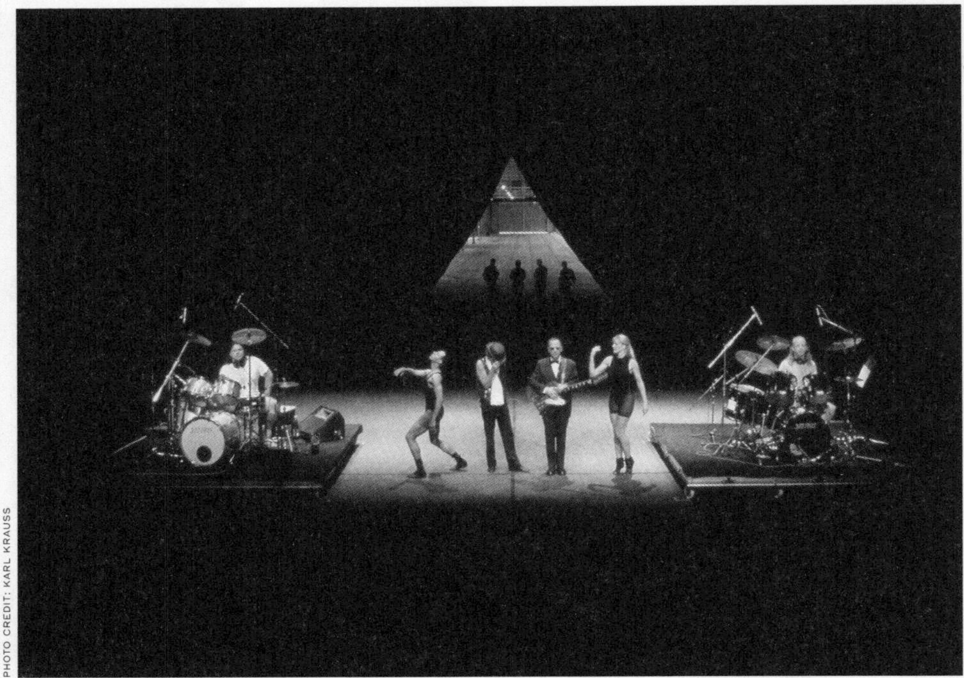

PHOTO CREDIT: KARL KRAUSS

Beat of the Traps, 1992
A work by Mike Kelley, Anita Pace, Stephen Prina
Choreography, composition, oration

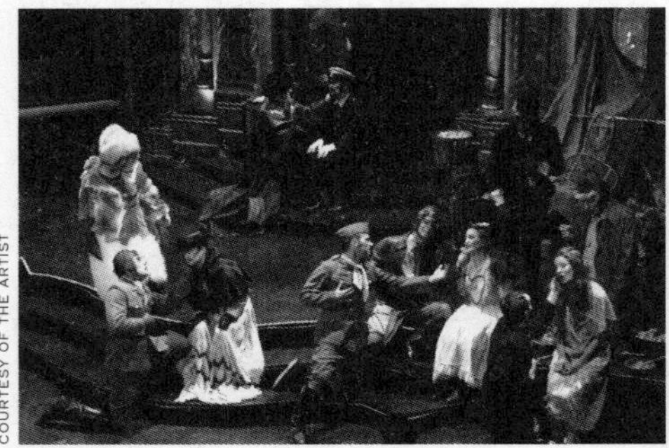

COURTESY OF THE ARTIST

Catherine Sullivan
Ice Floes of Franz Joseph Land (Orensanz Manifestation)
Performance view, Angel Orensanz Center, New York, April 10th 2004

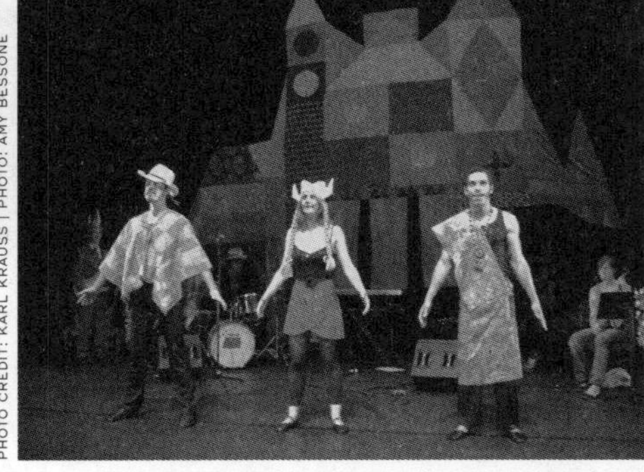

PHOTO CREDIT: KARL KRAUSS | PHOTO: AMY BESSONE

My Barbarian
MB: The Mary Blair Story, 2004
REDCAT, Los Angeles

piece was not a critical success, and even landed Satie in court, this sort of collaboration, quite contrary to the individualist mania that generally preoccupies studio artists, is the kind of work that inhabits the most productive of 20th-century breakdowns: the easing of borders between disciplines. Though such collaborations are not generally listed among the greatest achievements of otherwise identified artists, likely due in part to such work's awkward commodity status (the Nazis could not confiscate *Parade*, Sotheby's cannot auction it off, nor can MoMA hang it on any of its new walls), it is precisely this ambiguity that challenges the laws of bourgeois bohemia that experimental artists so fecklessly negotiate with the agents of capitalism. Descendants of this kind of work still provide luminous moments of rupture; I am imagining here *Beat of the Traps*, a 15-part performative collaboration devised by Stephen Prina, Mike Kelley, and Anita Pace in 1992, which created a conceptual mélange of art, music, dance, and theater. Though postmodernism relieved us of the burden of making new discoveries other than new combinations of old discoveries, such combinations can still be extremely energizing.

It is no accident that the stage is the place where Satie, Cocteau, Picasso, and Massine could come together, or that Prina, Kelley, and Pace found themselves collaborating there as well. Theater demands collaboration, and this is only the first of many reasons why theatrical conventions are so appealing these days to so many re-examinations of avant-garde principles. The idea that art does something, which is a conflicted notion in the history of visual expression, is at the core of theater, whose origins are in rituals that join social and aesthetic functions for the advancement of particular values and narratives. The ancient Egyptians performed coronation dramas that reenacted the struggles of their gods for religious and bureaucratic reasons, but also, one suspects, because everyone loves the spectacle of a show. Similarly, the Greek satyr plays developed into drama, allowing for mass investigation into the ethical questions of the day, laying familiar narratives upon a displaced and stylized set of regulated actions. European medieval pageant theater relied upon non-actor guildsmen to portray scenes from the bible for both instruction and festival entertainment on city streets. Here the blacksmiths' elaborate cart might have rolled along, depicting the fall from grace, followed perhaps by the leather workers, who could demonstrate Noah and his flood. In the theatrical traditions of both the East and the West, performance was used to create an allegorical space in which a communal investigation of social dynamics, not limited to professional artists, can take place.

Despite operating on opposite sides of the notion of realism, Brecht and Stanislavsky both updated this program in 20th-century terms, using the inherent displacements of theatrical presentation and its opposing, yet equally intrinsic aspect of unfolding narrative in a shared temporal space, to place this art between the individual's self-consciousness and his understanding of the reality that surrounds him. While contemporary theater as an institutional form has lost much of the urgency this practice can engender, theater as a framework for real-time exploration is valuable in a reality that grows less reliable year by year.

Specifically, artists who are organized around the visual are increasingly approaching theater as a means of cultural exploration that has a firmer "high-art" foundation than that which pop can provide. While young artists are expertly self-trained in pop culture and have been drawing on rock albums, television shows, and desirable celebrities ever since I've been paying attention, pop, in its never-ending cycle of empty self-affirmation, has produced a curious effect: its great irony is that irony itself is no longer ironic. To utilize a self-reflexive system self-reflexively is neither a great challenge to expectation, nor does it demonstrate any "true" rules of nature, which at least create a positive out of a double-negative. Born and bred on pop emptiness, younger artists are moving increasingly toward authenticity, however frailly it can be discovered. Here, theater, like other traditional arts and crafts, can provide a way out of pop's cycle of living death.

And when I use the term theater, I mean it as distinct from performance art, which has conventionally eschewed theatrical illusion and narrative in favor of a more sculptural sense of time and space. The body-art breakthroughs of Carolee Schneemann, for example, relied on treating the performing body in some sense as an abstract object, that is, as part of the same order of space that the viewer is sitting in, rather than confusing that space through presentational displacements (though I admit that the division I outline here is difficult to defend: some innovators of performance art like Eleanor Antin blurred this distinction from the start, and advanced multi-media practitioners like Matthew Barney presage an attractive yet scary permanent hybridization, which, incidentally, advances the system of art's commodification so that it may keep up with the times). The avant-garde strategy of defining non-art practices as art may have reached its apogee with performance art and the more performative aspects of conceptual art. After Adrian Piper and Sol LeWitt, the avant-garde dissolved into the great big pile of charming rubbish from which pastiche may forever emerge.

So, to reinvest this rubbish with some old-fashioned inspiration, non-art disciplines are being invaded by art, and theater, among those disciplines that are most due for dusting off, is now a place of experimental excitement. Notable in arranging this conflux is the artist Catherine Sullivan, whose performances and video projects amount to astute presentations of uncanny actors' workshops. I find Sullivan's work slightly brilliant, and I'm not alone in this judgment, though why exactly it is so appealing in my own view has much to do with my predilection for the theatrical form. Sullivan's *Ice Floes of Franz Joseph Land* (2003), a psychedelic-constructivist reinterpretation of the notorious Chechen rebels' siege of a Russian stage musical, perhaps the most bizarre contemporary episode of theater meeting life to produce cultural mayhem, has received much praise due to its formal ingenuity and its political cleverness. Sullivan, who has a background in both theater and fine arts, displays an interdisciplinary acumen that is bound to be quite influential; she is not merely a bored visual artist playing dress-up in the theater, but a technician skilled in both disciplines who brings them together to create an expanded vocabulary, both in visual and conceptual terms.

Sullivan's success as an artist mining theater for content and form is unusual, and again this returns us to the original problem: institutions are not built for interdisciplinary adventure. An art student cannot attend one of the MFA programs as they are currently structured and find a way to fulfill her studio requirements, as well as learn art history, plus theater history or music history or business or biology or string theory. An art school graduate may find it difficult to go to her gallery or best collector and explain that she needs a rehearsal studio for her new ballet. Nor can she go to the ballet world and expect her degree in sculpture to fling open the doors. In this sense artists, with their tradition of experimentation, continue to work on the front line, and find themselves responsible for creating the conditions in which to make the work they want to make.

This is where art institutions, especially MFA programs, must take the lead. In the face of capitalism's incorporative powers, the avant-garde failed to do anything substantial other than create markets for itself. Younger artists are often blamed for being unable to extend the fallacies that propelled the work that came before them, when in fact it was the grand delusions of modernism itself that made celebrity-geniuses of delightful crackpots and has now left us holding the bag. Yes, there is significant careerism and superfluity among the scores of grads who emerge from "top" MFA programs each year, as well as a lot of forgivable practical worries about paying off debt and validating one's work, but there is also rare genuine talent, intelligence, and an interest in doing something wonderful. The best and most useful thing we've inherited from modern art is the ability to dismiss formula. MFA programs in art, more so perhaps than those in other disciplines, should be able to draw on this hallmark of their form and broaden their curricula to include various histories and practices that will serve young artists well as they attempt to reach beyond reiterations of painting and sculpture. As so many faculty members at these schools have experimented themselves with other disciplines (recall the performative sculptures Charles Ray used to make, the art-rock of Mike Kelley and Mayo Thompson, the documented actions of Martin Kersels, Meg Cranston's plays, Simon Leung's opera, Ulysses Jenkins' videos, and Daniel J. Martinez's well-known participatory work, just to name a few) this kind of expanded pedagogy should not be such a stretch.

If graduate programs in art wish to strengthen their mission of educating students rather than simply preparing them to find galleries and court critics, then the sanctioned topics of discussion in art school should be expanded. I write specifically of theater here, as it is a neighboring field that is already being entered by clever artists, though I'd like to see others make cases for different interdisciplines. If the kinds of practices, theories, and histories that are explored in schools are multiplied, it might go a long way in dislodging the "crisis" in art that nostalgic experts are constantly lamenting, and the banal necrophilia that characterizes so much of the work that new artists make.

Notes

1
One of Marcel Duchamp's most extended discussions of his rejection of "retinal" art can be found in a conversation with Pierre Cabanne, "A Window onto Something Else," in Pierre Cabanne, *Dialogues with Marcel Duchamp* (New York: Viking, 1971), p. 43; see also Arturo Schwarz, *The Complete Works of Marcel Duchamp* (New York: Abrams, 1969), p. 18.

2
Clement Greenberg, "Abstract, Representational, and so forth," *Art and Culture* (Boston: Beacon Press, 1961), p. 135.

3
See Guy Debord, *The Society of the Spectacle* (New York: Zone Books, 1994), p. 72.

4
Filippo Tommaso Marinetti, cited in RoseLee Goldberg, *Performance Art from Futurism to the Present* (New York: Abrams, 1988), p. 17: "variety theater 'destroys the Solemn, the Sacred, the Serious, and the Sublime in Art with a capital A.'"

We Are All Conservatives ... or We are Dogs in Love With Our Own Vomit

Daniel J. Martinez

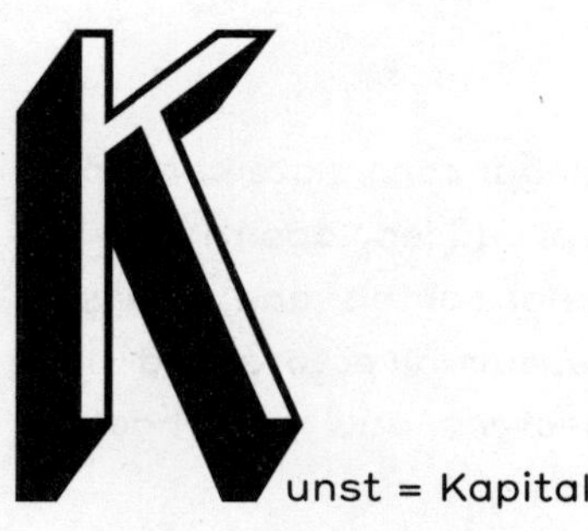

unst = Kapital
– Joseph Beuys, 1979

Carl Freedman	If you were asked to work on an advertising campaign for the Tories would you agree?
Damien Hirst	It depends on how much money.
Freedman	So you don't adhere to any particular political beliefs?
Hirst	That kind of integrity is bullshit. Nobody has that kind of integrity.
Freedman	You're not a socialist at heart?
Hirst	I'm not anything at heart. I'm too greedy ...

– *Supercollector: A Critique of Charles Saatchi*, 2000

Are you not ashamed that you give your attention to acquiring as much profit as possible and give no attention to truth and the perfection of your soul?
– Socrates, 399 BC

What is the appropriate response to a society of abundance?

The Dadaists and Surrealists did not consider themselves as producers of art or literature, but as revolutionaries, and the main intent behind their work was to change the world. The way they went about this was a matter of aptitude based in deep-rooted politics and philosophy. It produced a nihilism of generosity. Which in turn became hope.

If culture means the construction of empires, it also means the critique of them.

Today we are faced with a “new brand” called global corporate conceptualism—a dull, static, hyper-conservative, overproduced, apolitical, multinational art form maintained by the institutional cartels and mafias of established professionals (curators, critics, museum directors and their boards, biennials, art fairs, art magazines, collectors, and art schools).

The central dilemma: how is it possible to work outside of these despised values, systems, and structures while at the same time remaining sufficiently engaged to make a difference to them?

How is it possible to introduce a multiplicity of desires, which traverse and threaten the organizational relation to power, displacing the subject as a fundamental building block of capital and impassioned materialism.

How is it possible to escape the logic that consists in formulating one’s own disappearance or one’s own incapacity to produce meaning? (I repeat.)

How is it possible to escape the logic that consists in formulating one’s own disappearance or one’s own incapacity to produce meaning?

A number of the questions that haunted the 1980s and the culture wars of the 1990s seem to constitute vital issues today, maintaining multiplicity and simultaneity as a field of agency, integrating art, radical politics, and radical theory into parallel social systems, to form a-synchronous models of contemporary aesthetics.

Some of the questions that confront us are:

How can other modes of symbolic inscription and other forms of representation be conceived?

How can the events in which we are supposed to participate be translated into experience?

How can we represent ourselves in a history that is being written in terms of the economy, the free market, and the corporate museum?

How can the distance be reduced between the history that is being transmitted to us and the events that punctuate our daily lives?

How can we organize an evolving, radical democracy whose equilibrium is just and self-sustaining?

How can we represent our selves here and now?

How can we conceive of an emergent aesthetic?

We believe the moment of confusion is the precondition for the skepticism necessary for radical thought to become arenas for social experience.

To create and set in motion a series of tactics and subversions, reinvested with desire to organize a series of gestures that create a subjectivity, which produces, consumes, and yet it is neither passive nor obedient. Our intention is to sabotage the existing codes and decipher information, to render an ideological veil so we may forge our own language.

To sustain a praxis of radicality overthrowing the conditions and conventions of the boredom of everyday life. We embrace art, radical politics, and radical theory through a sustained practice of ontological anarchy and poetic terrorism.

Did you hear the invisible dragon has been slain. Hallelujah!

One Wind Tunnel, Eight Schools, 120 Artists

Yanira Cartageña

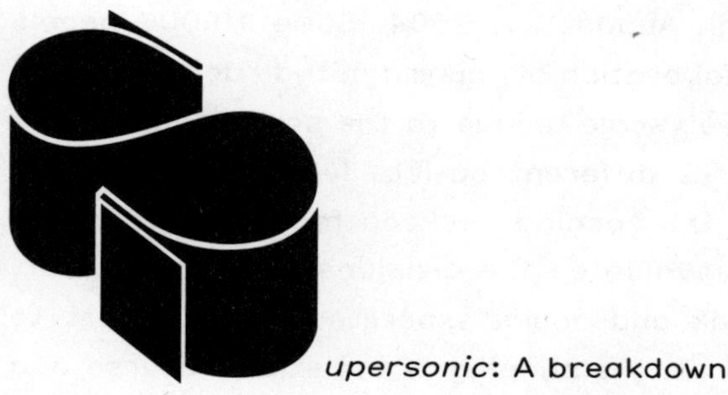

upersonic: A breakdown

In an effort to build a critical sense of community, eight graduate art departments from different institutions (Art Center College of Art and Design, the California Institute of the Arts, Claremont Graduate School, Otis School of Art and Design, UCLA, UC Irvine, UC San Diego, and USC) decided to create a unified event. Once the matter of which schools would participate and where the venue would be was decided, invitations were extended to the students of each program to organize the key aspects of the show. The main elements of the event consisted of a group exhibition and a catalog.

The concept for the show was generated shortly after a related initiative that sought to bring the same schools together for shared events, lectures, and symposia: the Southern California Consortium of Art Schools [SoCCAS]. SoCCAS has a faculty committee, with one member from each school. For the 2004 show, this overlapped with the *Supersonic* faculty committee, but is differently constituted in 2005. It also has a committee drawn from the diverse body of MFAs, MAs, and PhDs from each participating school. The mission of SoCCAS is centered on talks, discussions, and panels; but it also runs a website at www.SoCCAS.org; and, in partnership with JRP|Ringier, Switzerland, will publish the proceedings of its annual symposium, as in the present publication. In June 2004, the symposium, "Recent Pasts: Art in California from the 90s to Now" took place the day following the opening of *Supersonic*.

The *Supersonic* exhibition was installed in the newly renovated 16,000-square-foot former wind tunnel, originally constructed by the Jet Propulsion Lab of Cal Tech for space and aircraft research and development, but now part of Art Center's southern campus. The exhibition, titled *Supersonic: One Wind Tunnel, Eight Schools, 120 Artists*, opened June 12 and continued through August 21, 2004. Some 10,000 people turned up for the opening. Collaboration of this magnitude demonstrated the vibrancy, urgency, and sheer scale unique to the schools in the Los Angeles area. Through its three different outlets (exhibition, catalog, and symposium), the events of the opening weekend facilitated a crucial cross-institutional dialogue, reevaluated the divisions of cultural labor, and functioned as a think-tank and social experiment in an effort to articulate the role of education in the shaping of artistic discourse and practice.

The Space

The wind tunnel is a large cavern-like chamber where scale models (built to actual size) of airplanes were tested to determine the effects of wind pressure and resistance. As presented to the students, the space was an unfinished, virtually empty, 16,000 square foot giant chamber, with some additional floors and corridors in adjacent structures. An obvious immediate concern was that artwork might get lost in the architectural grandeur of the wind tunnel. But rather than let the space paralyze the works or installation, we embraced it as an asset. As large as the space was, it provided ample room and opportunity to locate a significant number of works, themselves very different in scale, address, and media.

The architectural space became the logical point of focus when deciding on the title for the show and the design of invitations, advertisements, and catalog. The student planning committee did not want to concentrate on any individual school or particular theme. For unless work was somehow classified according to imposed categories, any governing theme would be virtually unworkable—especially since the six-month time horizon made it impossible to circulate a call among the 120 artists for specially commissioned work that would fit a single brief. It was also decided early on that the focus would be on the MFAs as "emerging artists" rather than "graduating students." But in order to reflect the direction of the planning and organization of the show, some form of alternative focal point was needed. The history and layout of the wind tunnel became this de facto alternative. Formally a site of research and investigation, the wind tunnel would once again function as a location for exploration.

Planning

From conception to opening, the exhibition took some six months to come to fruition (a brevity almost unheard of in the professional museum or gallery world). Because of the pressure of time, the students formed three operating groups (each of which consisted of one representative from each school): the steering committee, catalog committee, and installation committee.

In an attempt to emphasize the event's collaborative nature and avoid the feel of trade show conventions, a steering committee was designed to direct the efforts of the different planning efforts (committees) and to coordinate the design and interior architecture of the exhibition space and placement of the work. These plans would later be handed off to the installation committee.

The catalog committee worked to complete a full-color catalog in time for the exhibition. The 80-page, full color, 9 x 12 inch publication featured all the artists plus writings from selected critics in the critical writing or Art History PhD programs of several schools.

The installation committee purchased and organized all the necessary equipment and tools to facilitate the mounting of the exhibition. During installation the committee coordinated the hanging and placement

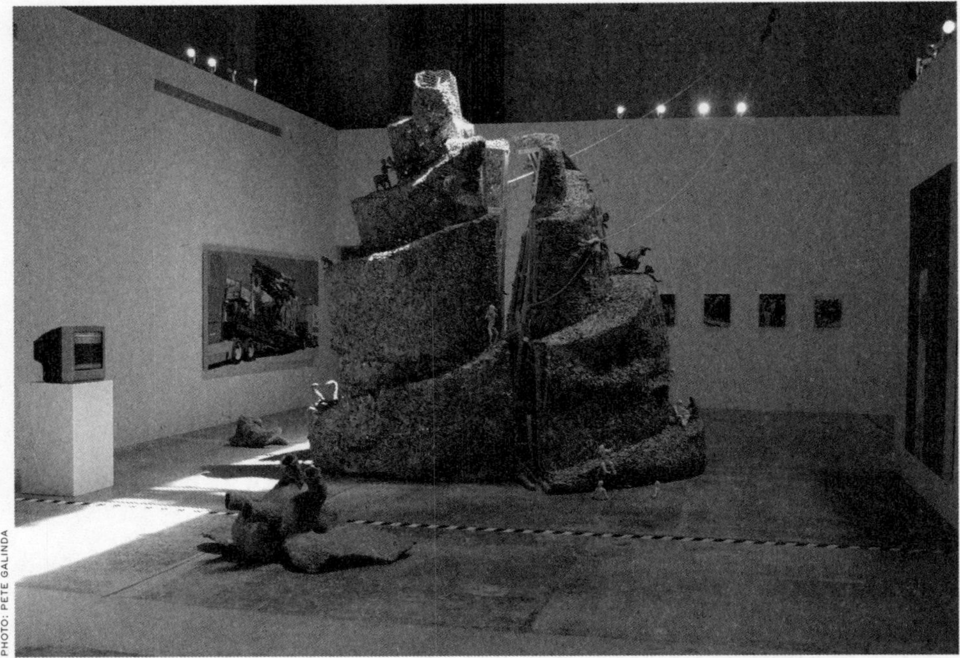

PHOTO: PETE GALINDA

Supersonic (One Wind Tunnel, Eight Schools, 120 Artists), 2004
Installation showing, center, Lindsay Brant's *The One Is Standing Apart From Me*, 2004
Art Center College of Design, Pasadena

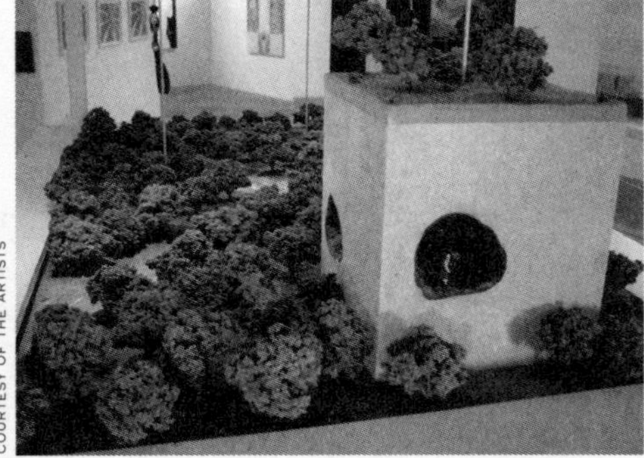

COURTESY OF THE ARTISTS

Patrick Marcoux and Ryan Taber
Orange Grove in Sepia: Grandpa Joad's Daydream, 2004
Installation View
Art Center College of Design, Pasadena

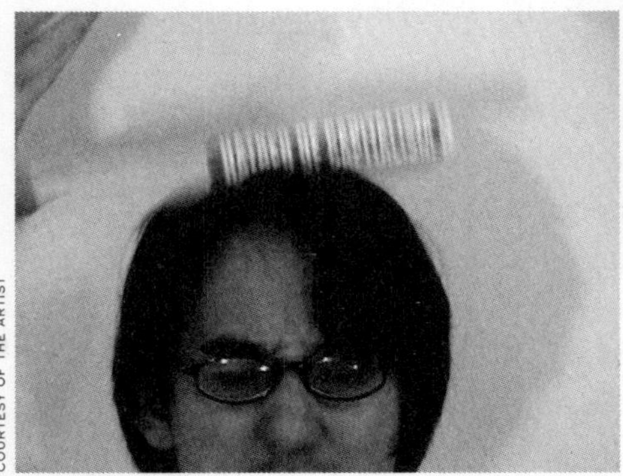

COURTESY OF THE ARTIST

Stephen Lam
Still from *In Advance of a Bruised Head from Desperate Attempts in Making Something Out of Nothing: Towards an Illegitimate Practice*, 2004
DVD, sound, color, 3:21 minutes.

of work and lights according to the installation plans and guidelines. They created a theater for screenings, facilitated work drop-off and pick-up, and accommodated artists working in different media with uniform shelving, projector shelves, and so on.

The planning committees operated in close communication with the MFA students at their respective schools. Therefore, all the participating artists involved had an opportunity to participate in planning and decision-making.

Organizing the Work

The students were particularly concerned with three things:

1. This was not to be a trade show, with parallel grid lines.

2. "Artist organized" does not equal a "disorganized mess." One could be creative with walls, angles, the positioning of the work—without installation taking precedence over the work itself. The work was definitely the most important thing for the planning committee.

3. There were very specific, technical aspects to be dealt with, including sound and light issues, and so on. Because of fire regulations, students were not allowed to put up ceilings over video works, which resulted in a whole new series of problems. We did not wish to isolate video work, but also did not want sound bleeding through to adjacent pieces. Some works needed natural light, others relative darkness for projection, while the paintings needed to be bathed in good even light.

In order to focus on works and the artists rather than schools and students, the submissions were not arranged by school, theme, or medium. Instead, so far as was possible, every artist's ideal work, space, equipment, and conditions were taken into consideration. Naturally, the need for compromise was obvious. Ideally, all artists should have been informed of any limitations and conditions ... to avoid surprises. But this became difficult because many decisions were taken out of the planning committee's hands. For example, one month before the show opened, two entire floors of the exhibition were suddenly unavailable, and work had to be uprooted. There were many things to contend with, each was addressed individually.

Expectations

The limitations of the show were apparent, almost from the get-go. There were issues of size and scale; the fact that the show was more self-selected than curated; as well as numerous other concerns. For example, some faculty members considered that a show of this size and level of exposure might compel recent graduates to present work that didn't represent what they might do in the future, or even what they were really making at the time. And that in certain cases, instant success might thwart or unduly pigeonhole an emerging artist.

But just as *Supersonic*'s limitations were obvious, so too were the inherent benefits for participating artists. The challenge of mounting a complex, large-scale exhibition in just under six months provided participants with an incomparable learning experience. The project launched a new tradition of collaboration and student leadership never before attempted in Southern California (or perhaps anywhere on this scale). Most importantly, because of the powerful list of guests and invitees, local and international curators, gallerists, and critics, *Supersonic* had an enormous potential to shape the future of arts locally, and to expand the influence of Southern California's emerging artists internationally.

These were the pros and cons of the show. The student committee was well aware of the implications, and cultivated competition that might result in such circumstances. One body of opinion felt that a sense of competitiveness was being exacerbated among the different schools and artists. Beginning with the initial choice of schools, and ending with the star-studded guest list and sheer scale of the opening, students were presented with an extraordinary opportunity, in a rich and diverse exhibition, which simultaneously became an amphitheater for competition.

The students, however, did not choose to exercise their competitive instincts. The planning committee concentrated on making the entire space flow, and giving each artwork the room to function on its own terms. Walls, rooms, and corners were built to accommodate specific pieces. Following the cues of students at each school, the reps were not really focused on concocting some weird, reality-TV show fostering head-to-head competition.

The spirit of collaboration extended even to the reviews. While individual viewers of the show might have chosen to speculate on the school-affiliation of any given piece, or made generalizations about "house-styles" and attitudes (there were clearly a lot of people who indulged in these guessing-games), on the whole, the show worked against such premises. It simply wasn't easy to apportion the work in this way; and many of those who started out doing this quickly gave up. Some critics did focus on individual artists. Christopher Knight (*Los Angeles Times*), Carrie Patterson (*Flash Art*), and Jan Tumlir (*Artforum*), all mentioned between three and seven artists whose work was of particular interest to them; but they did not comment on them as representatives of a school-generated style. School affiliations were usually marked in parentheses, but no serious publication pitted the schools against each other.

While the participating artists worked hard to make the entire show function and flow as a whole, everyone was aware of the presentation of *Supersonic* as a "land of plenty" for up-and-coming artists. During the planning stages, one of LA's senior artists, John Baldessari, was quoted as saying: "Finally it is happening ... an exhibition of graduating MFA students in LA from not one school but many. What a pay off! The possibility to compare and assess, the ante will sure rise, as will the competition and resulting art." The stage was set for grandiose daydreams of art-stardom, and collector courtship and, yes, even a kind of benign competition was fostered ... if not quite advocated.

Some artists chose to address these issues directly. An obvious example was the collaborative team of Patrick Marcoux and Ryan Taber, who created *Orange Grove in Sepia: Grandpa Joad's Daydream*, which stood at the center of the wind-tunnel space. Among its other implications, this installation clearly takes on the expectations generated by the show. The piece itself is a large, science-center-type structure that houses a small-scale sculptural depiction of an abundant landscape where opportunities to survive and flourish hang from the trees and even wait in hidden caverns beneath the ground. The landscape of abundance and plenty is composed of details imagined by the members of the Joad family during their migration from dustbowl Oklahoma to California's bountiful Central Valley. The representation of these fantasies is based on John Steinbeck's Depression-era novel, *The Grapes of Wrath* (1939) in which a family's dreams of verdant fruit orchards and ample employment opportunities later prove to be delusions. Most artists, in fact, realized that *Supersonic* was a provisional destination for them, and that the show was just one of many stepping-stones in their career.

Beyond expectations of competition and the sense of prodigious possibilities, for those already critical of the graduate school training process there was also the expectation that Supersonic might come across as the culminating moment for graduate students steered into a market-focused art world (on the model of big show = possible gallery representation = success). Anyone who has been in grad school for a while is familiar with the position sometimes advocated there that students are in training for their future marketability, that their work may suffer (or "succeed") in consequence, that young artists are in many ways disenfranchised, and—beyond this—that there is an overabundance of galleries and a relative lack of alternative spaces.

Jan Tumlir, points out in the "Best of 2004" (*Artforum*, December 2004), that "*Supersonic* inspired much talk of selling out and reignited the late-90s art-school controversies." "But," he continued, "considering that a good number of the show's works were already signed-off to local galleries and, moreover, that none of its participants seemed genuinely determined to resist a similar fate for their art, these complaints seemed more than ever tinged with sour grapes." Articulating a well-supported response to the art school controversy, his article actually reinforces the futility of the "sell out" argument, as he mentions several artists that interest him and in parenthesis identifies to which gallery each has signed on.

Another opinion that emerged from criticism of the exhibition is that by no means all of the artists in *Supersonic* were interested in resisting a gallery-oriented future. Some artists responded directly to the commercial prospects of the show. The artist collective, Superflunk, for example, produced a series of concert-style T-shirts offered for sale within the wind-tunnel space. During the opening the "seemingly authentic *Supersonic*" T-shirts were sold inside the exhibit at a price of $15.00. Outside, "scalpers" sold "rip-off *Supersonic* T-shirts" for $10.00. There were a variety of T-shirts available, all commenting on the show as spectacle, on careerism in the arts, and on consumerism and celebrity. One had Baldessari's quote (see above) printed on the front side. Another spelled out "STAR" with a connect-the-dots made up from the word “Supersonic.” Yet another was emblazoned with: “I was an artist at *Supersonic* and all I got was this lousy T-shirt.” Throughout the duration of the show *Supersonic* T-shirts were bought and sold, but in the end all of the profits were stolen from Superflunk’s display.

Yet another response to generalizations about success, venue, and consumerism is to challenge the familiar binary of gallery system vs. alternative art, altogether. By forcing work into a space in which it does not easily belong many artists argued, implicitly and explicitly, against the familiar dichotomy of “outside” and “inside.” Instead, the parameters of gallery art itself must be challenged. Many artists in *Supersonic* worked with this approach in mind, including Xavier Cha. In *Topiary Tags* Cha uses a hedger to sculpt her name, “Xavier,” raised-up and clearly visible, into shrubs and bushes around Los Angeles. Cha documents her “topiary tags” in video and identifies their location around the city. Sometimes the tags have been sculpted into the gardens of affluent areas where graffiti would not normally last an hour. The fact that she is able to “sneak in” a tag, where it would normally not survive, begs the question of what belongs where, and why a gardener is more invisible than a graffiti artist in such neighborhoods. Work like this might begin to challenge the very definitions and parameters of the communities it inhabits.

In *Notes on Desperate Attempts in Making Something Out Of Nothing (toward an illegitimate practice)* (2004), Steven Lam ultimately creates work that functions inside a gallery—but at the same time challenges the parameters of art practice, post-studio practice, and the art school itself. The piece is made up of 23 short video works. Everyday, for a month, Lam attempted to record an impromptu action in order to make a distinction between work and labor. He refers to Pierre Bourdieu’s claim that “the games of artists and aesthetes and their struggle for the monopoly of artistic legitimacy are less innocent than they seem. At stake in every struggle over art there is also the imposition of an art of living that is the transmutation of an arbitrary way of living into the legitimate way of life which casts every other way of living into arbitrariness.” He references pop culture and political theory, and employs slapstick as a way to critique commodity fetishism.

Conclusion

Whatever importance this show had or will have will not really be clear until the artists in it have moved their work and their lives to other places. But we truly feel that one of the most significant things about *Supersonic* is that it existed so vividly at its own particular moment, a moment deeply shared between 120 artists in Southern California in the summer of 2004.

List of Contributors

ANNE BRAY

LA Freewaves executive director Anne Bray has been working in the field of media arts since the mid-1970s as an art teacher, administrator, and artist. After receiving her MFA from UCLA in 1985, she worked until 1989 as the coordinator of LACE's [Los Angeles Contemporary Exhibitions] pioneering video exhibition, archives, workshop, and access programs. She founded LA Freewaves and has administered the program since its inception in 1989. Bray teaches at Claremont Graduate University and the University of Southern California. Her own artwork has been exhibited widely.

CORNELIA (CONNIE) H. BUTLER

Connie Butler is a curator of contemporary art at the Museum of Contemporary Art, Los Angeles. Since 1996 she has organized numerous exhibitions and publications including *Robert Smithson* (2004) co-curated with Eugenie Tsai; *Rodney Graham: A Little Thought* (2004-2005); *Flight Patterns* (2000–2001) and *Afterimage: Drawing Through Process* (1999). She is currently working on a major international survey exhibition of feminist art, *WACK! Art and the Feminist Revolution*, scheduled to open at MOCA in 2006, as well as retrospective exhibitions with the American artist Dan Graham and the South African artist Marlene Dumas. Prior to her current position Butler was Curator of Contemporary Art at the Neuberger Museum of Art, Purchase, New York, and curator at Artists Space, New York. She has lectured and published extensively on post-war contemporary art.

YANIRA CARTAGEÑA

Yanira Cartageña is an artist working in installation and media who graduated from the MFA program at the California Institute of the Arts, Valencia, in 2004. She was chair of the student organizing committee for *Supersonic*, the exhibition of graduating work by some 120 artists from the art programs at eight Southern California schools.

MATTHEW COOLIDGE

Matthew Coolidge is Director of Programming for the Center for Land Use Interpretation (CLUI), Venice, California. CLUI is a programming and research organization dedicated to investigating the nature and extent of human interaction with the earth's surface. Its members and affiliates fulfill this mandate by embracing multidisciplinary approaches, including conventional research and information processing methodology as well as the use of nontraditional interpretive tools. Founded in 1994, the organization has produced over 30 exhibits on land-use themes and regions for numerous public institutions in the United States and internationally. Coolidge has curated many of the exhibits created by the Center over the past ten years, including *Hinterland* (Los Angeles Contemporary Exhibitions, 1997), *Commonwealth of Technology* (List Center for Visual Arts at the Massachusetts Institute of Technology, 1999), and *The Nellis Range Complex: Landscape of Conjecture* (CLUI, Los Angeles, 1999). He is the author of several books published by CLUI, including *The Nevada Test Site: A Guide to the Nation's Nuclear Proving Ground*, *Around Wendover: An Examination of the Anthropic Landscape of the Great Salt Lake Desert Region*, and *Route 58: A Cross-Section of Southern California*. Coolidge has been investigating land use issues since studying environmental science and contemporary art at Boston University (BA 1991), and has furthered his research into human-induced changes to the landscape since becoming the Director of Programming at the foundation of CLUI in 1994. Under his direction the Center has received numerous grants and awards, including from the Andy Warhol Foundation for the Visual Arts, and the National Endowment for the Arts. He lectures widely about the activities of the Center, and is a faculty member of the curatorial studies program at the California College of Art.

MEG CRANSTON

Meg Cranston is a Los Angeles-based artist, writer, curator and the founder of the Open Field Museum. Her work has been shown in museums and galleries internationally. Recent exhibitions include *A Walk to Remember* (curated by Jens Hoffmann), Los Angeles Contemporary Exhibitions (2004); *Volcano Trash and Ice Cream* at the Happy Lion Gallery, Los Angeles; and museum exhibitions at Museum für Gegenwartskunst, Siegen, Germany and K21, Düsseldorf. Her writings have been published in numerous journals including *ArtText* and *ArtUS*; and she is a former editor of *JOURNAL: A Contemporary Art Magazine*, and co-editor (with Hans-Ulrich Obrist) of a forthcoming collection of writings by the artist John Baldessari. Together with Baldessari, she has curated several exhibitions including *100 Artists See God*, which traveled in the US and Europe, 2004–05. Cranston is a professor of art and criticism at Otis College of Art and Design.

TEDDY CRUZ

Teddy Cruz' work dwells at the border between San Diego, California and Tijuana, Mexico, where he has been developing a practice and pedagogy that emerge out of the particularities of this bicultural territory and the integration of theoretical research and design production. He has a Masters in Design Studies from Harvard University and was awarded the Rome Prize in Architecture from the American Academy in Rome. Cruz has been recognized internationally for his collaborations with community-based nonprofit organizations such as Casa Familiar and for work on housing and its relationship to urban policies that are more inclusive of social and cultural programs. He is currently an associate professor in public culture and urbanism in the Visual Arts Department at UCSD in San Diego. He received the 2004-05 James Stirling Memorial Lecture On The City, an international Prize in Urbanism co-organized by the Canadian Center of Architecture, the Van Alen Institute in New York City and the London School of Economics and Political Science.

MALIK GAINES

Malik Gaines is a writer, curator, and performer based in Los Angeles, who has contributed to numerous magazines and journals, including *ArtUS*, the Los Angeles-based magazine which he co-founded and co-edits. He has written cataloge essays for shows including *Gary Simmons* at CAIS Gallery in Seoul, South Korea, and *Freestyle* curated by Thelma Golden for the Studio Museum in Harlem, which garnered attention and criticism for introducing the term "Post-Black," and still generates discussion.

Gaines' curatorial projects include *To Be Recycled* at Six Months Gallery, Los Angeles, and the multi-sited survey exhibition *Fade*, the first part of the City of Los Angeles' *African American Artists in Los Angeles* (2003-2004), which appeared at The Craft and Folk Art Museum, the Luckman Gallery, and The University Fine Arts Gallery at Cal State, LA. Gaines' work in theater and performance includes a new play commissioned by the Mark Taper Forum, and ongoing music and theatrical gigs performed collaboratively with his band, My Barbarian. A recipient of a Penny McCall Foundation award in 2003, Gaines teaches writing at Cal State Fullerton, and is currently teaching graduate courses at the San Francisco Art Institute. Gaines earned an MFA from the CalArts School of Critical Studies and has already emerged as a key voice in the articulation of recent developments in the art world of Southern California.

RITA GONZALEZ

Rita Gonzalez is a video maker, independent curator, and writer based in Los Angeles, whose artwork has been shown at the Canal Isabel II (Spain), the Armand Hammer Museum (Los Angeles), Bronx Museum (New York), Self-Help Graphics (East LA), the Center on Contemporary Art (Seattle), and at international festivals. Together with Norma Iglesias, she curated a film and video series for inSITE2000, the bi-national exhibition staged between San Diego and Tijuana. Her co-curated collaboration, *Mexperimental Cinema*, the first survey of experimental and avant-garde work from Mexico traveled to the Pacific Film Archives; the Museum of Contemporary Art, San Diego; Harvard Film Archives; the Guggenheim Museums (New York and Bilbao); and was featured in film festivals internationally.

Gonzalez has written for media and art journals including *The Spectator*, *Wide Angle*, *Poliester*, *COIL*, *Signs*, and *Latinart.com*. She is currently co-editing *Pedacitos de mi corazón: Selected Writings of Tomas Ybarra-Frausto* (with Chon Noriega) for the University of Minnesota Press; and finalizing her doctoral dissertation in the Department of Film, Television, and Digital Media at UCLA. She is Assistant Curator and Special Assistant to the Deputy Director at the Center for Art of the Americas, Los Angeles County Museum of Art.

NORMAN KLEIN

Norman Klein studies how consumer spectacle and confused urban planning hide social conditions, as in Coney Island where he grew up, and various neighborhoods around downtown Los Angeles, where he has lived since 1973. He has expanded these interests into two series of books, one on cultural histories of forgetting, that commenced with *The History of Forgetting: Los Angeles and the Erasure of Memory* (Verso, 1997), another on the history of special-effects environments that gave rise to *The Vatican to Vegas: The History of Special Effects* (New Press, 2004). He has recently completed the second volume of the history of forgetting, *Bleeding Through: Layers of Los Angeles, 1920–86* (2003) a database novel mixing printed text with DVD-ROM (nominated for the Image Award at Transmediale in Berlin). He is also author of *Seven Minutes: The Life and Death of the American Animated Cartoon* (Verso, 1996).

Klein is currently researching for another database novel and museum show, *The Imaginary Twentieth Century*, which address how audiences walk through false memories of the future. His forthcoming novella, *Freud in Coney Island and Other Tales* was featured in a retrospective of his work at the Beall Center at UC Irvine (2004). Klein has taught at many of the consortium schools, including Art Center, Pasadena, UCSD, USC, UCLA, and CalArts, where he is on the faculty of the School of Critical Studies.

ERIK KNUTZEN

Erik Knutzen is a program developer at the Center for Land Use Interpretation, and has collaborated on the research and production of a number of the Center's exhibitions and programs including *On Locations: Places as Sets in the Landscape of Los Angeles*, *Ground Up: Photographs of the Ground in the Margins of Los Angeles*, and *Emergency State: First Responder and Law Enforcement Training Architecture*. Knutzen has applied a background in video production and interdisciplinary research to the Center's unique objectives.

DANIEL J. MARTINEZ

Daniel J. Martinez is an artist based in Los Angeles. His work incorporates a wide range of media including sculpture, video, animatronics, siteless activities, and site-based actions, engaging social, political, and art-world structures with pointed criticality and frequently dark humor. His solo exhibitions include shows at the Project, Los Angeles (2002) and New York (2001, 1999); the Museo de Arte Alvar y Carmen T. de Carrillo Gil, Mexico (2001); Orchard Gallery, Derry, Ireland (2000); The Three Rivers Art Festival Gallery, Pittsburgh (2000, 1998); and Artspace, Auckland, New Zealand (1995, 1996).

His work has been included in many group shows including the Lima Biennial, Lima, Peru (2002); *Seeing* at the LACMA Lab, Los Angeles (2001); *Made in California, 1900–2000*, at LACMA; *East of the River* at the Santa Monica Museum of Art (2000); the Whitney Biennial (1993); and the Venice Biennial (1993). Since 1988, Martinez has worked extensively in the arena of public art, including projects initiated with the Veteran's Hall of Los Angeles (2000); the Three Rivers Arts Festival (1996); the City of Philadelphia (1993); a procession, carnival, parade, and installation for Culture in Action, a Public Art Program in Chicago (1993); and *Le Démon Des Anges*, which included billboards installed in San Diego, Lyon, Nantes, Barcelona, and Stockholm (1990). His public art projects include several collaborations with Renee Petropoulos and Roger White. Martinez has received numerous awards and distinctions including a Pollock-Krasner Fellowship (2001), a City of Los Angeles COLA Individual Artist Fellowship (2000), a J. Paul Getty Fellowship for Individual Artists (1997), and the National Endowment for the Arts Individual Artist Fellowship in New Genres (1995 and 1989). Martinez teaches at the University of California, Irvine (UCI).

DAVE MULLER

Based in Los Angeles, artist and DJ Dave Muller's recent solo exhibitions include *Dave Muller: Connections* at the Armand Hammer Museum (LA) and the Center for Curatorial Studies Museum, Bard College, New York (2002); *Spatial* at the Saint Louis Art Museum (2001); *How to Secede (Without Really Trying)* at The Approach, London (2000); as well as frequent shows at Murray Guy gallery in New York and Blum & Poe gallery in Santa Monica and Los Angeles. Muller has participated in numerous group exhibitions including the 2004 Whitney Biennial. His work explores the often amorphous boundary conditions between artist and curator, and high art and commercial advertising. Among his many activities with sound and image he produces "Three-Day Weekends," which he describes as "an artist-run nomadic project," as well as watercolor, pencil, and ink drawings based on actual exhibition announcements. The wryly humorous hand-made posters and art magazine covers, advertising other artists' work, are a witty investigation of the contemporary art scene and its promotional systems. Muller's ongoing series of drawings are inspired by amateur flyers created by fans of indie-rock bands and many other cultural sources.

MARCOS RAMÍREZ (ERRE)

Marcos Ramírez (ERRE) is an artist and activist operating from the border of Mexico and the US. ERRE was born in Tijuana, Mexico, in 1962 and received a Law degree from the Universidad Autonoma de Baja California, Tijuana, Mexico, in 1982. ERRE's artistic practice engages a diverse group of traditional and new media, and involves gallery work as well as public art projects. He has exhibited throughout Mexico and in the United States since 1993, and his solo shows include *Jardin de los Angeles/Garden of Angels* at Quint Contemporary Art in La Jolla (2002), and *LA Multiplication de los Panes/The Multiplication of Bread* which has been exhibited at multiple sites including La Mesa College Gallery in San Diego (2004), the Iturralde Gallery, Los Angeles (2003), and Intersection for the Arts in San Francisco (2002). He has also participated in numerous group exhibitions including *Away From Home*, Wexner Center for the Arts, Columbus, Ohio (2003); *Mixed Feelings: Art and Culture in the Postborder Metropolis*, USC Fisher Gallery in Los Angeles (2002); *Lateral Thinking: Art of the 1990s*, Museum of Contemporary Art, San Diego (2001); *Made in California*, Los Angeles County Museum of Art (2000); the Whitney Biennial (2000); the 6th and 7th Havana Biennials (1997 and 2000); and inSITE94 and 97. Recently, ERRE's work was included in the traveling exhibition *Baja to Vancouver: West Coast Contemporary Art* which showed at the Seattle Art Gallery, CCA Wattis Institute for Contemporary Art, the Vancouver Art Gallery, and the Museum of Contemporary Art, San Diego.

OSVALDO SÁNCHEZ

Cuban-born curator and art critic, Osvaldo Sánchez is currently Artistic Director of inSite_05. Co-Curator of inSITE2000, he also served as Director of the Museo de arte contemporáneo interacional Rufino Tamayo (2000, Mexico City); Director of the Museo de arte Carrillo Gil (1998–2001, Mexico City); and Director of the Fourth and Fifth International Forum for Contemporary Theory (FITAC, Guadalajara, Mexico, 1995–1996). Sánchez was a columinst for *Reforma* (Mexico City, 1994–96) and has published numerous articles and essays about Mexican and Latin American art. He has participated in international conferences and has lectured extensively at venues including Bard College (New York), the Guggenheim Museum (New York), the America's Society (New York), the Museo de arte Reina Sofia (Madrid, Spain), the University of Texas, Austin, and the University of California, San Diego. Sánchez has received grants from the American Foundation (2000) and the Fideicomiso Rockefeller-Bancomer-FONCA (1999).

FRANCES STARK

Frances Stark is a visual artist and writer, whose books include *The Architect and the Housewife* (Book Works, 1999) and *Collected Writing: 1993–2003* (Book Works, 2003), which includes essays on the work of a wide range of innovative contemporary artists, many of them based in Southern California: Allen Ruppersberg, Laura Owens, Bas Jan Ader, Michael Lin, Jorge Pardo, Olafur Eliasson, Raymond Pettibon, and Kevin Hanley. The book also includes catalogue essays written for the Walker Art Center's *Painting at the Edge of the World* (2000), and *Circles: Socializing, Networking & Peer-Grouping in Contemporary Art* (Revolver, Frankfurt, 2003), as well as nine shorter pieces originally published from 1999 to 2001 in her *Art + Text* column "type." Stark also writes fictional prose, poetry, and statements connected to her own visual art practice, some of which are included in these anthologies.

As an artist she has put on some 18 solo gallery exhibitions since 1991 and two solo museum exhibitions, at the Armand Hammer Museum in Los Angeles (*The "Unspeakable" Series*, 2002) and the Kunstverein in Munich (*Ich Suche Nach Meine Frances Starke Seite*, 2000). She has been represented by the galleries Marc Foxx in Los Angeles and CRG in New York since 1996, greengrassi in London since 1998, and Galerie Daniel Buchholz in Cologne since 2000. Her work can be found in numerous public collections.

JOHN C. WELCHMAN

SoCCAS founding chair, John C. Welchman is Professor of art history and theory in the Visual Arts department at the University of California, San Diego. He is the author of *Modernism Relocated: Towards a Cultural Studies of Visual Modernity* (Allen & Unwin, 1995), *Invisible Colours: A Visual History of Titles* (Yale UP, 1997), and *Art After Appropriation: Essays on Art in the 1990s* (Routledge, 2001); co-author of the *Dada and Surrealist Word Image* (MIT Press, 1987) and of *Mike Kelley* in the Phaidon Contemporary Artists series (1999); and editor of *Rethinking Borders* (Minnesota UP, 1996). He has written for *Artforum* (where he had a column in the late 1980s and early 1990s), *Screen, Art + Text, Third Text*, the *New York Times*, *International Herald Tribune*, the *Economist*, and other newspapers and journals; and contributed cataloge essays for exhibitions at Tate (London and Liverpool), Reina Sofía (Madrid), Museum of Contemporary Art (Los Angeles), the LA County Museum of Art, the Sydney Biennial, Vienna Museum of Contemporary Art, and the Ludwig Museum (Budapest).

His current projects include editing the collected writings of Mike Kelley (the first volume, *Foul Perfection: Essays and Criticism*, was published with MIT Press in 2003; the second, *Minor Histories*, also, with MIT, arrived Spring 2004; volumes on music and sound culture, interviews and performance scripts are in preparation). Welchman is finalizing two books on the relation between art, film, and the representation of faces (*The Celluloid Face* and *Faces and Powers*); and is contracted to write a major survey, *World Art Now* for Phaidon (London).

HOLLY WILLIS

Holly Willis is the editor of *RES Magazine*, a bimonthly publication devoted to innovations in film, video, music, and design. She also co-curates RESFEST, a traveling festival of shorts, design films, and music videos, and writes frequently on experimental media. Her column "Signal to Noise" in the *LA Weekly* covers local video art, and she has recently completed a book manuscript on emerging digital cinema to be published by Wallflower Press. In addition to editing and writing, Willis also teaches classes on critical thinking and the histories of film and video.

This book is the first volume of the Southern California Consortium of Art Schools [SoCCAS] symposia. The inaugural symposium was held on June 13, 2004, in the Silver Screen Theater at the Pacific Design Center, Los Angeles, in collaboration with the Museum of Contemporary Art, Los Angeles.

EDITOR John C. Welchman
EDITORIAL COORDINATION Clare Manchester
EDITING + PROOFREADING Clare Manchester
PICTURE EDITING Julia Dzwonkoski
COVER IMAGE Jennifer Pastor
The Perfect Ride, 2003 (detail)
polyurethane and steel,
46 1/2 x 26 x 10 inches
Courtesy Regen Projects, Los Angeles
DESIGN Gavillet & Rust
ASSISTANCE Fabian Monod
PRINTING Musumeci SpA
TYPEFACE Hermes (www.optimo.ch)

The publication has received generous support from the founding member schools of SoCCAS: Art Center College of Art and Design, Pasadena; California Institute of the Arts, Valencia; Claremont Graduate School; Otis College of Art and Design; University of California, Irvine; University of California, Los Angeles; University of California, San Diego; and the University of Southern California.

Printed in Europe.

ISBN 3-905701-20-0

PUBLISHED BY
JRP|Ringier
Letzigraben 134, CH-8047 Zurich
T +41 (0) 43 311 27 50
F +41 (0) 43 311 27 51
www.jrp-ringier.com
info@jrp-ringier.com

JRP|Ringier books are available internationally at selected bookstores and the following distribution partners:

SWITZERLAND
Buch 2000, AVA Verlagsauslieferung AG,
Centralweg 16, CH-8910 Affoltern a.A.,
buch2000@ava.ch, www.ava.ch

FRANCE
Les Presses du réel, 16 rue Quentin,
F-21000 Dijon, info@lespressesdureel.com,
www.lespressesdureel.com

GERMANY AND AUSTRIA
Vice Versa Vertrieb, Immanuelkirchstrasse 12,
D-10405 Berlin, info@vice-versa-vertrieb.de,
www.vice-versa-vertrieb.de

UK
Art Data, 12 Bell Industrial Estate,
50 Cunnington Street, London W4 5 HB,
info@artdata.co.uk, www. artdata.co.uk

USA
D.A.P./Distributed Art Publishers, 155 Sixth
Avenue, 2nd Floor, New York, NY 10013,
dap@dapinc.com, www.artbook.com

OTHER COUNTRIES
IDEABooks, Nieuwe Herengracht 11,
1011 RK Amsterdam, idea@ideabooks.nl,
www. ideabooks.nl

For a list of our partner bookshops or for any general questions, please contact JRP|Ringier directly at info@jrp-ringier.com, or visit our homepage www.jrp-ringier.com for further information about our program.